Promises kept

THE WHOLE STORY
OF THE BIBLE

by Carl Laferton

Promises kept
The good book guide to the whole story of the Bible
© The Good Book Company, 2012
Reprinted 2013
Series Consultants: Tim Chester, Tim Thornborough,
                    Anne Woodcock, Carl Laferton

The Good Book Company
Tel (UK): 0345 225 0880
Tel (int): + (44) 208 942 0880
Tel: (US): 866 244 2165
Email: info@thegoodbook.co.uk

Websites
UK: www.thegoodbook.co.uk
N America: www.thegoodbook.com
Australia: www.thegoodbook.com.au
New Zealand: www.thegoodbook.co.nz

ISBN: 9781908317933

Printed in China

CONTENTS

Introduction 4

Why study Promises Kept? 5

1. A very good world: Creation 7
Genesis 1 – 2; John 1

2. Broken by rebellion: The fall 13
Genesis 3; Luke 11

3. Covenant made: Abraham 19
Genesis 12, 21; John 8

4. Delivered from judgment: The exodus 27
Exodus 12; Luke 22

5. Ever-reigning king: King David 35
Judges 2; 2 Samuel 7; Mark 8 – 9

6. Future beyond judgment: The prophets 43
Amos 8 – 9; Luke 23

7. God in His world: Jesus of Nazareth 51
Luke 9, 24

8. Hear the message: Today 59
Acts 1 – 2

9. In a perfect world: Jesus' return 67
Revelation 20 – 22

Leader's Guide 73

introduction: good book guides

Every Bible-study group is different—yours may take place in a church building, in a home or in a cafe, on a train, over a leisurely mid-morning coffee or squashed into a 30-minute lunch break. Your group may include new Christians, mature Christians, non-Christians, mums and tots, students, businessmen or teens. That's why we've designed these *Good Book Guides* to be flexible for use in many different situations.

Our aim in each session is to uncover the meaning of a passage, and see how it fits into the "big picture" of the Bible. But that can never be the end. We also need to appropriately apply what we have discovered to our lives. Let's take a look at what is included:

⊕ **Talkabout:** Most groups need to "break the ice" at the beginning of a session, and here's the question that will do that. It's designed to get people talking around a subject that will be covered in the course of the Bible study.

⊕ **Investigate:** The Bible text for each session is broken up into manageable chunks, with questions that aim to help you understand what the passage is about. **The Leader's Guide** contains **guidance on questions**, and sometimes ⊗ additional "follow-up" questions.

⊕ **Explore more (optional):** These questions will help you connect what you have learned to other parts of the Bible, so you can begin to fit it all together like a jig-saw; or occasionally look at a part of the passage that's not dealt with in detail in the main study.

⊕ **Apply:** As you go through a Bible study, you'll keep coming across **apply** sections. These are questions to get the group discussing what the Bible teaching means in practice for you and your church. ⊕ **Getting personal** is an opportunity for you to think, plan and pray about the changes that you personally may need to make as a result of what you have learned.

⊕ **Pray:** We want to encourage prayer that is rooted in God's word—in line with his concerns, purposes and promises. So each session ends with an opportunity to review the truths and challenges highlighted by the Bible study, and turn them into prayers of request and thanksgiving.

The **Leader's Guide** and introduction provide historical background information, explanations of the Bible texts for each session, ideas for **optional extra** activities, and guidance on how best to help people uncover the truths of God's word.

why study Promises Kept?

One Saturday, less than a decade after the end of Jesus of Nazareth's life, a man named Paul stood up in a Jewish synagogue with a mind-blowing message.

"We tell you the good news," he said. "What God *promised* our ancestors, he has *fulfilled* for us, their children, by raising up Jesus" (Acts 13 v 32-33).

In many ways, in these two sentences Paul was summing up the story of the whole of the Bible.

The God Paul was talking about is a *promise-making* God. Throughout history, he has made huge, extravagant, wonderful promises to humanity. We find many of those promises in what he said to the ancestors of the members of that synagogue—what he said to men such as Adam, Abraham, David. And as we see what God did, we see the shape of how he will fulfil what he has said.

Because, crucially, God is also a *promise-keeping* God. What he says, he does. And at a particular point in history, he fulfilled all of his promises in the life, death, resurrection and rule of one human—Jesus, a carpenter from a small Jewish town.

The Bible tells the story of what God promised. And it tells the story of how God has fulfilled those promises.

And so it's the story of the *good news*—the gospel. It's the story of how God has been at work for people, through people, and often despite people—and supremely it's the story of how he worked through one Person, Jesus.

This Good Book Guide will take you on a rapid tour of the whole story of the Bible. There won't be time to stop at every sight—only to point out some of the highlights. Over nine sessions, you'll travel from the beginning of the past, through our present, to the future.

Each session, you'll see what God promised, and something of how his promise was fulfilled. And each session, you'll be given a snapshot, an image which sums up that period of time. Put them all together and you'll have an album detailing the whole of history—the whole story of God's promises, and how he has fulfilled them in Jesus.

It's a whirlwind tour. It's a breathtaking tour. And it's a tour we're part of...

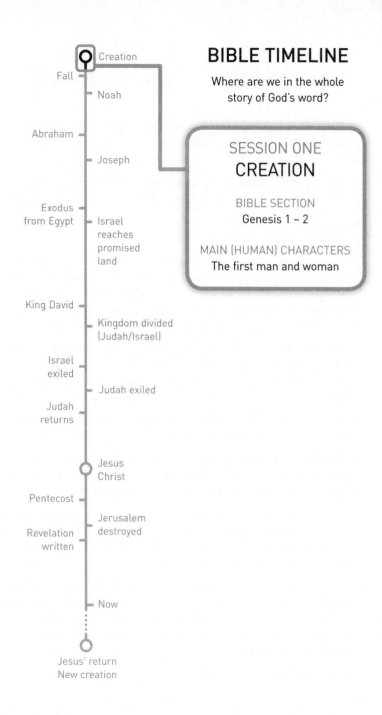

BIBLE TIMELINE

Where are we in the whole story of God's word?

Creation

Fall

Noah

Abraham

Joseph

Exodus from Egypt

Israel reaches promised land

King David

Kingdom divided (Judah/Israel)

Israel exiled

Judah exiled

Judah returns

Jesus Christ

Pentecost

Jerusalem destroyed

Revelation written

Now

Jesus' return
New creation

SESSION ONE
CREATION

BIBLE SECTION
Genesis 1 – 2

MAIN (HUMAN) CHARACTERS
The first man and woman

1

Genesis 1 – 2; John 1
A VERY GOOD WORLD
CREATION

⊕ talkabout

1. What is the most naturally beautiful or spectacular part of the world you've seen? How did visiting it make you feel?

What God promised...

⊥ investigate

> **Read Genesis 1 v 1-25**

We are looking right back to "the beginning" (v 1): the very start of the world's history.

2. What did God do (v 1)?

    • How did he do it (v 3)? What does this show us about what he is like?

3. Split into pairs or small groups. Pick two or three of these sections each to have a look at: Genesis 1 v 6-8, 9-13, 14-19, 20-23.
    • What is happening in each of the sections you've looked at?

• What similarities do you see between them?

4. What have we learned about God?

▶ Read Genesis 1 v 26 – 2 v 3

5. What is the last thing that God made?

• What is different about how this part of his creation is described? What does this mean, do you think?

• What job does God give them (v 28)?

6. What is God's verdict on his creation (v 31)?

⊡ apply

7. How does humanity's place in creation...
 • make us humble?

 • make us valuable?

 • give us purpose in life?

8. There are many issues in society today where knowing we are creatures, made in God's image, to rule his world, should shape our view. Pick a few now, and discuss what Genesis 1 v 26-31 has to say about them.

⊡ getting personal

Are there any areas in your life where you need to be reminded that you're not God, not in overall charge?

Where do you get your sense of value from? The shifting opinions of others, or the changing foundation of your looks, career, or health? What would change in your emotions and outlook if you based your identity on being made and valued by God?

What would change if your main purpose each day was to know God, live under his rule, and work in his world as he directs you?

SNAPSHOT: Genesis 1 – 2

The people God made enjoy perfect life with each other, under his rule, in his very good world.

The implicit promise of Genesis 1 – 2 is that the creation will be "very good" (1 v 31). That is what God says this world will be like. BUT today, our world is only a poor reflection of the world as it was created. Can the world God promised be recovered, or has his plan gone wrong?

... *He has fulfilled*

⬇ **investigate**

▶ **Read John 1 v 1-5, 9**

9. What similarities are there between these verses and Genesis 1 v 1-5?

10. What do we learn about "the Word"?

11. **Read verse 14.** What is amazing about these words?

- God's word brought light to creation (Genesis 1 v 5)—here, the Word became flesh to bring "light", too. What is that "light" (John 1 v 4)?

- This Word was called Jesus (v 17). And John wants us to see that Jesus' coming is where God begins "creating" again. How is God "creating" through Jesus coming to earth?

getting personal

God's children (John 1 v 12) are not only part of his original creation, but also part of his new creation, begun when the Word became flesh to bring the light of life to the world.

What difference does that make to your life? Do you think about what can be enjoyed in this world too much, or too little? Do you care for it too much, or too little? Do you think of your future as part of God's re-creation too much, or too little?

pray

Praise God...

that he is the Creator, and for making you to enjoy life in his creation. that he sent Jesus to bring life and begin recreating this imperfect world.

Confess to God...

ways you make too much, or too little, of his world.

Ask God...

to help you to be humble, to find your value in being made by God, and to live as he created you to each day (you might want to pray for specific ways in which you need his help in doing these things).

explore more

optional

Genesis 2 focuses on the climax of God's creation: humanity.

▶ **Read Genesis 2 v 18-25**

What is "not good"? What does God do about it (v 21-22)?

The man responds with a love song (v 23—you may not rate it much!).

What relationship have they been made for (v 24)?

What kind of relationship do they enjoy in God's creation (v 25)?

What do these verses tell us about men and women?

BIBLE TIMELINE

Where are we in the whole
story of God's word?

Creation

Fall

Noah

Abraham

Joseph

Exodus
from Egypt

Israel
reaches
promised
land

King David

Kingdom divided
(Judah/Israel)

Israel
exiled

Judah exiled

Judah
returns

Jesus
Christ

Pentecost

Jerusalem
destroyed

Revelation
written

Now

Jesus' return
New creation

SESSION TWO
THE FALL

BIBLE SECTION
Genesis 3 – 11

MAIN CHARACTERS
Adam and Eve
Cain and Abel
Noah

2 BROKEN BY REBELLION

Genesis 3; Luke 11

THE FALL

The story so far

The people God made are enjoying perfect life together under his loving rule in his very good world.

⊕ talkabout

1. As you look at the world today, in what ways is it still "very good", as God created it? In what ways isn't it?

   • What reasons do people give for the world not being "very good"?

What God promised...

⊕ investigate

> **❯ Read Genesis 3 v 1-6**

2. What do the woman and the man, who God created, do?

• **Read Genesis 2 v 15-17.** What is so serious about their actions?

3. What tactics does the snake—the devil—use as he tempts the woman?

4. What is it that convinces the woman and the man to disobey God (v 5-6)?

⊟ apply

5. How do we experience the same tactics when the devil tempts us?

⊡ getting personal

Like our ancestors, we're all tempted to follow the devil and disobey God. If we don't realise we're being tempted, we're already giving in.

How are *you* regularly tempted to disobey the God who made you, in your attitudes or in your actions? Does the devil suggest you should doubt God's words (v 1); that he doesn't mean what he says (v 5); or that he doesn't know what's best for you (v 5)?

⊡ investigate

This pair had rejected God's rule, his right to say what is right and wrong in his world. They had tried to make themselves their own gods. But no matter how hard humans try to do that, nor how many of them do that, God is still God. And he does not let rebellion against him go unjudged...

> **Read Genesis 3 v 7-24**

6. What effect does rejecting God and deciding to make the rules themselves have on the man's and woman's...
  - relationship with each other (v 7, end v 16—look back at 2 v 25 to compare)?

  - relationship with God (v 8, 23)?

  - relationship with God's world (v 17-19)?

  - future (end v 19, v 24)?

  - How do we see these effects in the world today?

7. Think about what humans had been created to enjoy in God's creation. How are these verses a reversal of those things?

8. Look at what God says to the snake in verses 14-15. What promise does God make (v 15)?

  - How does this give hope to humanity?

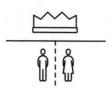

SNAPSHOT: Genesis 3 – 11

The people God made are now shut out from his presence, have imperfect relationships with each other, and live in an imperfect world, facing death.

The only hope for humanity is God's promise. From Genesis 3 onwards, we are searching for the woman's offspring, the one who can and will defeat the devil and free humanity from his power—from death.

... *He has fulfilled*

⊕ investigate

❯ Read Luke 11 v 14-22

9. What is Jesus doing (v 14)?

Some bystanders think Jesus is working for the devil, "Beelzebul" (v 15).

10. What answer does Jesus give (v 17-19)? Far from working for the devil, what does he say he has come to earth to do (v 20)?

• Jesus' mini-story (v 21-22) explains his miracle (v 14). Who is the "strong man" (v 21)? Who's the "someone stronger" (v 22)?

11. How is Jesus the fulfilment of the promise of Genesis 3 v 15?

⊒ apply

12. From this session and the last one, how would you explain to a friend…
 • what our world is like, and why?

• what humans are like, and why?

• how the problems of the world and humanity can be fixed?

⬆ pray

Confess to God that, like our first ancestors, you're sinners. Acknowledge (out loud or in your hearts) specific ways you've disobeyed him this week.

Thank God that he does not leave us where we deserve, under the power of the devil, but instead came as Jesus to free us.

Ask God to help you notice when you're being tempted, and give you the strength to resist the devil and know the blessing of living God's way.

⊡ explore more

optional

> **▸ Read Genesis 11 v 1-9**

What do people decide to do, and why (v 1-4)?

God had told humanity to "fill the earth" (1 v 28). What do these people think of God's plan (v 4)?

What ends up happening, and why (v 8-9)?

How is this historical episode similar to what happened in Genesis 3?

What are we seeing about what God is like? And about what humans are like?

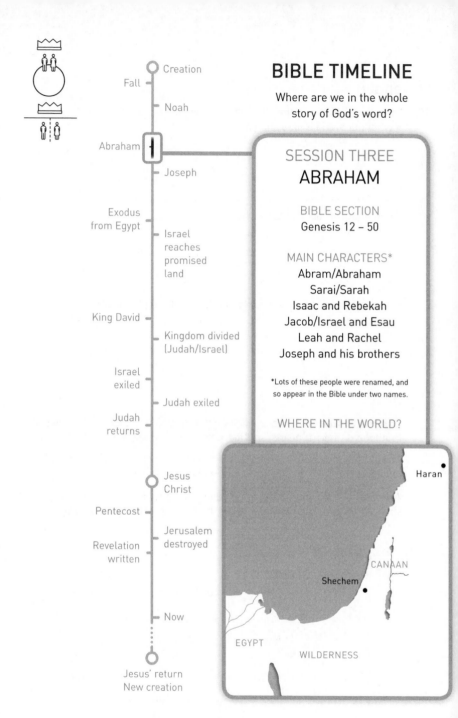

BIBLE TIMELINE

Where are we in the whole story of God's word?

Creation
Fall
Noah
Abraham
Joseph
Exodus from Egypt
Israel reaches promised land
King David
Kingdom divided (Judah/Israel)
Israel exiled
Judah exiled
Judah returns
Jesus Christ
Pentecost
Jerusalem destroyed
Revelation written
Now
Jesus' return
New creation

SESSION THREE
ABRAHAM

BIBLE SECTION
Genesis 12 – 50

MAIN CHARACTERS*
Abram/Abraham
Sarai/Sarah
Isaac and Rebekah
Jacob/Israel and Esau
Leah and Rachel
Joseph and his brothers

*Lots of these people were renamed, and so appear in the Bible under two names.

WHERE IN THE WORLD?

Haran
CANAAN
Shechem
EGYPT
WILDERNESS

3 COVENANT MADE

ABRAHAM

The story so far

Humans have rejected God's rule and come under the captivity of the devil. They now have no relationship with God, imperfect relationships with each other, and live in an imperfect world, facing death.

⊕ talkabout

1. What, if anything, would persuade you to move away permanently from your...
   • country?
   • friends?
   • family?

What God promised...

⊕ investigate

▶ **Read Genesis 12 v 1-7**

2. What did God tell Abram to do (v 1)?

3. What did he promise Abram?
- v 1:

- v 2:

- v 3:

Since Genesis 3, humans have been waiting for the man who will defeat the devil, returning humanity to blessing. Now we find that God intends to use a member of Abram's family to bring that blessing to "all peoples on earth" (v 3). The Bible calls his promises to Abram a "covenant": a binding agreement (see Explore More at the end of this session).

From this point in history, we need to look at Abram's descendants for the One who will fulfil God's promise back in Genesis 3. Unsurprisingly, the rest of the Bible story is about Abram's family, and how God blessed all peoples through one of his descendants.

These verses therefore give us a great lens through which to read the rest of the Old Testament. Whichever part we're reading, we should ask:
- *How is God at work to bring his people (Abram's descendants) to his land where they can live under his blessing?*
- *Are we being told anything about what the blessing-bringing descendant will be like, or what he will do?*

4. How does Abram respond (v 4)? How is this a great example of real faith?

- Look back at **Genesis 11 v 29-30**, and compare it with 12 v 2. Why is Abram's response to God's promises particularly impressive?

Abram made many mistakes. But he continued to show this kind of faith. And by trusting in God's promises, he enjoyed the blessing of life in right relationship with God. Genesis 15 v 6 puts it this way: "Abram believed the LORD, and he credited it to him as righteousness".

➔ apply

5. If we have real faith, as Abram did, how will it show itself in our lives?

6. In Abram's time, land, community and family were what people looked to for security in life. What are the things people look to for security today?

• Where should the Christian look? Why is this hard?

⊡ getting personal

What do you value most? Your possessions, family, career, comforts... or your relationship with God? If God were to call you to "leave ... and go", what would you find hardest to leave behind? That's the thing that is most likely to be, or become, an idol to you—something you love and worship instead of God.

⊡ investigate

Years pass. Sarah, Abraham's infertile wife, reaches her nineties (Genesis 17 v 17). God's promise of children is more impossible than ever...

❯ **Read Genesis 21 v 1-7**

7. What do we learn from this episode about how God works?

SNAPSHOT: Genesis 12 – 50

From Abraham, God will make a people, living in his land, under his rule and blessing. And through one of Abraham's descendants God will bless people throughout the world.

...He has fulfilled

⊕ **investigate**

❯ **Read John 8 v 31-44**

8. It's 1800 years later, and Jesus is talking to members of Abraham's family tree. But what problem do they all have (v 34-35a, 44)?

• What do they need Jesus, God the Son, to do for them (v 36)?

• What do they want to do with Jesus (v 40)? What does this show about them (v 39)?

9. How are they different to Abraham (v 40—think back to how Abraham reacted to God's words in Genesis 12)?

The conversation continues…

> **Read verses 54-59**

10. What does Jesus say Abraham did while he was still alive (v 56)?

We've seen that God promised that he would bring blessing to people from all over the earth through one of Abraham's descendants (Genesis 12 v 3). This is what Abraham was rejoicing at the thought of.

• So what claim is Jesus making for himself in John 8 v 56? What should we expect to see Jesus doing?

⤵ **apply**

11. Who, today, are the true children of Abraham (v 39, 56)? (Galatians 3 v 29 may help you here.)

12. Imagine someone said to you: "Of course I'm a Christian. I've been baptised. I was born into a Christian family. I go to church." What does John 8 have to say about this view?

⬆ pray

Thank God for...

Ask God for help with...

⦂ explore more

optional

> **Read Genesis 15 v 1-21**

Which two of his promises does God underline here (v 4-5, 7)?

Notice again the crucial detail in verse 6—that it's Abram's trust in God fulfilling his promises that makes him right with God. But still, as Abram points out in verse 8, can he really know all this will happen?

God responds by telling Abram to set up the traditional area where binding agreements are made (v 9-11). Usually, both parties would pass through the pieces of dead animals, to show what should happen if they broke the agreement. Here, only God, made visible as fire, does (v 17). This agreement is *all* about what *God* will do.

What further prediction and promise does God make (v 13-16)?

What does the writer call this binding agreement that God makes with Abram (v 18)?

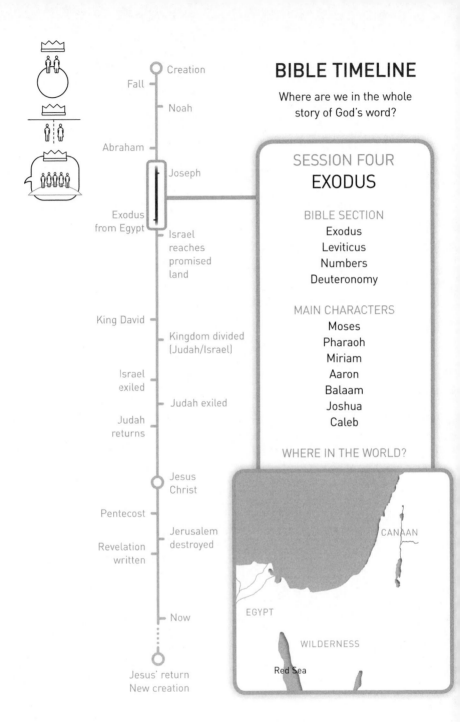

BIBLE TIMELINE

Where are we in the whole
story of God's word?

Creation
Fall
Noah
Abraham
Joseph
Exodus from Egypt
Israel reaches promised land
King David
Kingdom divided (Judah/Israel)
Israel exiled
Judah exiled
Judah returns
Jesus Christ
Pentecost
Jerusalem destroyed
Revelation written
Now
Jesus' return
New creation

SESSION FOUR
EXODUS

BIBLE SECTION
Exodus
Leviticus
Numbers
Deuteronomy

MAIN CHARACTERS
Moses
Pharaoh
Miriam
Aaron
Balaam
Joshua
Caleb

WHERE IN THE WORLD?

CANAAN

EGYPT

WILDERNESS

Red Sea

4 Exodus 12; Luke 22
DELIVERED FROM JUDGMENT
THE EXODUS

The story so far

From Abraham and his descendants, God has promised to make a people, living in his land, under his rule and blessing. And through one of Abraham's descendants, God has promised to bless people throughout the world.

⊕ talkabout

1. Imagine you surveyed 100 people in your area and asked:
   • What is the biggest problem you face?
   • Is there a solution to that problem, and what is it?
   What answers would you get, do you think?

What God promised...

⊕ investigate

What we've missed: Abraham's grandson was Jacob. One of Jacob's sons was Joseph, who ended up second-in-command of Egypt. After a while, the whole family joined him there.

In Exodus 1, a new king (or pharaoh) came to power. He saw that the Israelites (Jacob's family) had become "exceedingly fruitful" and "numerous" (v 7), and he viewed them as a threat. So he enslaved them, and killed all their newborn sons.

One boy, Moses, escaped the killings. And as an adult, God appeared to him and made a promise...

> Read Exodus 3 v 7-10

2. What does God promise Moses he will do?

• What does the Israelites' greatest problem appear to be? What solution does God offer?

Pharaoh refused to listen to Moses; he said: "Who is the LORD, that I should obey him and let Israel go? I do not know the LORD" (5 v 2).

Even though God showed him who he was by sending nine plagues, Pharaoh still resisted. So God promised Moses: "I will bring one more plague on Pharaoh and on Egypt. After that, he will let you go" (11 v 1). We pick up the story as Moses tells God's people what the LORD has told him to tell them...

> Read Exodus 12 v 1-13

3. What do the Israelites need to do?
• v 3-5:

• v 6-7:

• v 8-10:

• v 11:

4. Why do they need to do this (v 12-13)?

• So what is really the Israelites' greatest problem? What is the solution that God offers?

> **Read Exodus 12 v 28-30**

5. What do the Israelites do (v 28)?

• What does God do (v 29)?

• What does Pharaoh do (v 30-32)?

6. Verse 30 tells us: "There was not a house without someone dead". But in Israelite houses, the firstborn sons had been spared! So how is this verse correct?

• What does this show about how God rescues people from his judgment?

⤳ **apply**

7. From this study, and the previous ones, what is humanity's greatest problem? Where must we look for the solution?

▣ **getting personal**

Our prayers for ourselves and our loved ones are a good reflection of what we really think we, and they, need.

Do you pray first and foremost each day that you would keep looking to God to rescue you from his judgment? What about those you know who aren't looking to God to rescue them—is your main prayer for them that they would do so?

SNAPSHOT: Exodus – Deuteronomy

God has rescued Israel from Egyptian slavery and from his judgment, making them his people and leading them towards the land he has promised to give them.

⊡ **investigate**

▶ **Read Exodus 12 v 14-27**

8. What should the people do after their rescue (v 14, 17, 24-25)? Where will they do this, and what should they remember (v 25-27)?

For 1400 years, God's people living in his land (which came to be called Israel) shared this meal, called both "Passover" (v 11) and the "Festival of Unleavened Bread" (v 17), every year. It was the same every time, right down to the words that were said when the bread was eaten and the wine was drunk, all looking back to God's amazing rescue of his people from Egypt.

Until, at a Passover meal in Jerusalem, a descendant of Abraham said some very different words…

…He has fulfilled

▶ **Read Luke 22 v 7-20**

9. How many times is the word "Passover" mentioned in v 7-13? Why does the writer, Luke, do this, do you think?

10. During the meal, Jesus takes the bread (v 19) and the wine (v 20) that were part of the way Israel looked back to the Passover in Egypt. But what does he say they now represent?

- Whose blood does Jesus point his followers to? Link this back to the events of Exodus. What does this blood achieve?

- Where is the "land" where Jesus is looking forward to eating the Passover meal (v 16, 18)?

11. What does Jesus tell his followers to do (v 19)? How do his people do this in practice today?

⊡ apply

The Passover in Moses' day was a wonderful shadow—but still only a shadow, of the greater Passover achieved by Jesus.

12. Use the events of the Passover in Egypt to explain to someone else in the group what Jesus achieved on the cross.

13. What should we be thinking about, and how should we be feeling, when we share Communion?

↑ **pray**

Thank God for...

Ask God for help with...

⊡ **explore more**

optional

God, just as he had promised (3 v 12), brought his people to Mount Sinai (also called Horeb), on their way to the promised land. And there God spoke to Moses...

▶ **Read Exodus 20 v 1-17**

We tend to call this section the Ten Commandments. But before telling the people what he wants them to do, God *first* points out something that he has *already* done.

What is it (v 2)?

What comes first—being rescued by God, or obeying him? Why is this crucial to remember?

Read through the Commandments. Which does your society generally agree with, and which does it reject?

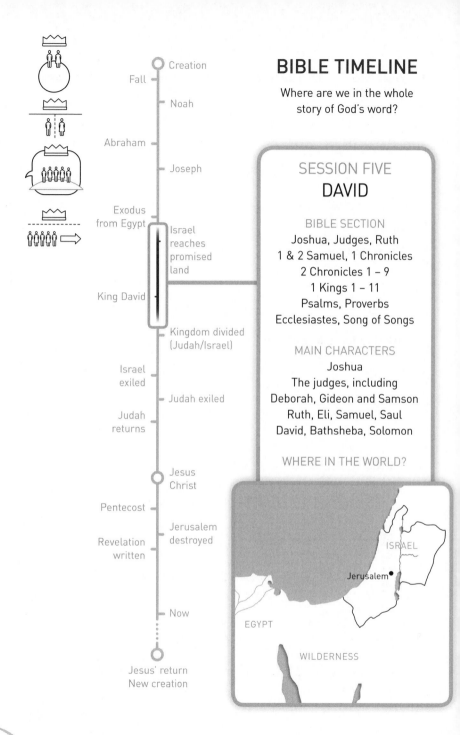

Creation

Fall

Noah

Abraham

Joseph

Exodus
from Egypt

Israel
reaches
promised
land

King David

Kingdom divided
(Judah/Israel)

Israel
exiled

Judah exiled

Judah
returns

Jesus
Christ

Pentecost

Jerusalem
destroyed

Revelation
written

Now

Jesus' return
New creation

BIBLE TIMELINE

Where are we in the whole
story of God's word?

SESSION FIVE
DAVID

BIBLE SECTION
Joshua, Judges, Ruth
1 & 2 Samuel, 1 Chronicles
2 Chronicles 1 – 9
1 Kings 1 – 11
Psalms, Proverbs
Ecclesiastes, Song of Songs

MAIN CHARACTERS
Joshua
The judges, including
Deborah, Gideon and Samson
Ruth, Eli, Samuel, Saul
David, Bathsheba, Solomon

WHERE IN THE WORLD?

ISRAEL

Jerusalem ●

EGYPT

WILDERNESS

5 EVER-REIGNING KING

KING DAVID

The story so far

God has rescued Abraham's descendants, Israel, from slavery in Egypt, and from his judgment. He did it by giving them a lamb to die in their place. They have left Egypt to travel to the land he has promised them.

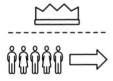

⊕ talkabout

1. Have you ever found yourself making the same mistake repeatedly, even though you resolve each time not to do it again?

- What made it so hard to stop? What would have helped you?

What God promised...

⊕ investigate

What we've missed: Under Moses, God brought Israel to the brink of the land he'd promised to give them. Because of the people's refusal to trust and obey God as they travelled through the desert, he kept them from entering the land for 40 years. But under Moses' successor, Joshua, Israel finally came into it, and defeated the peoples living there.

God's people are now in God's land enjoying the blessing of living under his rule. Things are going really well...

>> Read Judges 2 v 6-19

2. What happened after Joshua died?
   • Verses 10-13:

   • Verses 14-15:

   • Verse 16:

3. What was the advantage of having a God-given judge (v 18)?

   • What was the problem (v 19-21)?

In the book of Judges, this cycle repeats itself time and time again. The people sin; God allows their enemies to occupy the land; the people cry out to God; he raises up a judge to rescue them; they enjoy God's blessing under the judge; the judge dies and the cycle starts again. Each time the cycle goes round, things get a little worse, and never quite return to being as good as they were.

4. **Read Judges 17 v 6; 18 v 1; 19 v 1; 21 v 25.** What does the writer of Judges suggest is the basic cause, and the solution to, Israel's troubles?

⊡ apply

5. What does Judges 2 (and the whole book) tell us about what God's people are like?

• Do we see this today? How?

6. What does it tell us about the benefits and limitations of human leaders?

⊡ getting personal

Are you turning a blind eye to sin in your church, and then wondering why God doesn't bless you with growth? Are you turning a blind eye to your own sin, and wondering why things aren't going as you hoped?

It's wonderful that, when we see our sin, we can cry out to God for rescue, and he will forgive us and bless us. Do you need to do so now?

⬇ investigate

What we've missed: God gave his rebellious people a king. The first, Saul, was the king they deserved: he rejected God's commands. The second, David, was a king they didn't deserve. He was God's "anointed one", his "Messiah" or "Christ". David loved God, tried to obey him, and sought forgiveness when he disobeyed. He led the people in trusting in and obeying God.

Under David, Israel enjoyed God's blessing in God's land under the rule of God's chosen king. In many ways, it was the high point of Israel's history. But of course, David was just a man…

❯ Read 2 Samuel 7 v 4-16

7. What will happen to David himself (v 12a)? Why does this matter (Hint: Think back to the problem with the judges)?

8. But what does God promise about one of his descendants?
• Verse 12:

• Verses 13, 16:

• Verses 14-15:

• What else does God promise David (v 10-11)?

Verses 10-11 are a promise God partially fulfilled in David's time. But they were also pointing forward to what God's people would enjoy under the reign of David's never-dying descendant, the "Messiah" or "Christ" of God, in his never-ending kingdom.

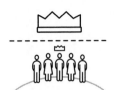

SNAPSHOT: Joshua – 1 Kings 11

God's people are living in God's land, under God's king, who leads them in living under God's rule. But their persistent sin prevents them from fully enjoying God's blessing.

...He has fulfilled

⊥ investigate

▶ Read Mark 8 v 27-29, 9 v 2-10

9. What does Peter recognise about Jesus?

10. How does 9 v 2-8 show that Peter is right?

• Given what God promised David, why is this seriously exciting?!

11. Remember, the central flaw with both the judges and with David is that, though they may lead God's people to obey God for a while, eventually they die. Why is what Jesus foretells in verse 9 so crucial?

⊟ apply

12. Why is it good to obey Jesus? Why is it right to do so? Why do we find it hard to?

⊡ getting personal

Re-read Mark 9 v 2-9. Is this the Jesus you know? Is your view of who he is big enough, or is it limited to friend, guide, teacher? How would your thinking and your conduct in the coming week change if you always listened to Jesus as the Messiah, the Son of God?

↑ pray

Thank God...

• that he does not give his people what they deserve, but rescues them.

• for the leaders of your church, denomination and state. Pray that God would use them to implement his laws, to protect the vulnerable, and to enable his word to be heard.

Ask God...

• to help you not make too much of leaders, nor too little of them.

• to show you where you are living as you "see fit", instead of how he commands, and to change you so that you would know the blessing of obedience.

optional

⊡ explore more

Solomon, David's son, succeeded him as king.

❯ Read 1 Kings 4 v 20-34

Remember God's promises to Abraham of people, land and blessing to all nations, as well as his promise to David of an everlasting King and kingdom.

*Pick out the verses which suggest Solomon might be **the** Messiah, the fulfilment of God's promises.*

❯ Read 1 Kings 11 v 1-13

What happened to Solomon (v 1-8)?
How did God react (v 9-13)?

David was not the Messiah. Nor was Solomon. Nor were any of the other kings of Israel. Few encouraged the people to live under God's rule: and all died. For centuries, God's people waited for God's chosen King…

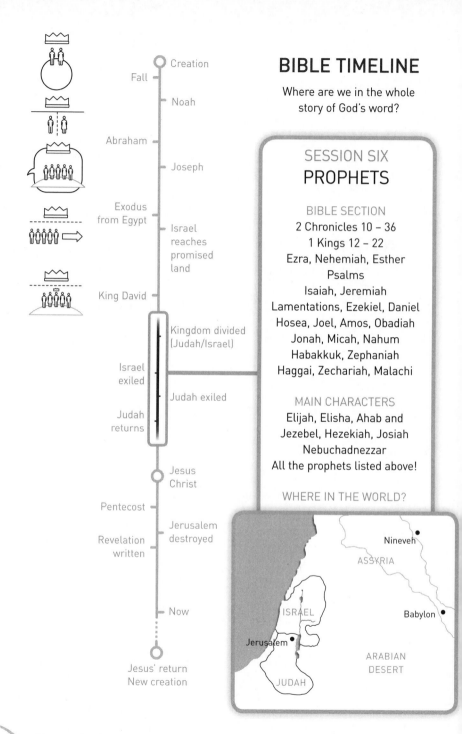

BIBLE TIMELINE

Where are we in the whole
story of God's word?

Creation
Fall
Noah
Abraham
Joseph
Exodus
from Egypt
Israel
reaches
promised
land
King David
Kingdom divided
(Judah/Israel)
Israel
exiled
Judah exiled
Judah
returns
Jesus
Christ
Pentecost
Jerusalem
destroyed
Revelation
written
Now
Jesus' return
New creation

SESSION SIX
PROPHETS

BIBLE SECTION
2 Chronicles 10 – 36
1 Kings 12 – 22
Ezra, Nehemiah, Esther
Psalms
Isaiah, Jeremiah
Lamentations, Ezekiel, Daniel
Hosea, Joel, Amos, Obadiah
Jonah, Micah, Nahum
Habakkuk, Zephaniah
Haggai, Zechariah, Malachi

MAIN CHARACTERS
Elijah, Elisha, Ahab and
Jezebel, Hezekiah, Josiah
Nebuchadnezzar
All the prophets listed above!

WHERE IN THE WORLD?

Nineveh
ASSYRIA
ISRAEL
Babylon
Jerusalem
ARABIAN
DESERT
JUDAH

6 FUTURE BEYOND JUDGMENT

Amos 8 – 9; Luke 23

THE PROPHETS

The story so far

In God's land, God's people kept rebelling, and so kept being invaded instead of enjoying blessing. God gave them judges to rescue them, and has now appointed King David, who has led the people into obedience and blessing.

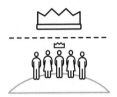

⊕ talkabout

1. What do you most look forward to in life?

• How does that affect your feelings and actions in the present?

What God promised...

⊥ investigate

What we've missed: David's son, Solomon, worshipped other "gods", not the real one. Sin brought judgment: when he died, the kingdom split in two—"Israel" in the north; "Judah" in the south. Most kings did as Solomon had, and the people increasingly rejected God and his ways.

So God spoke to them through his prophets. There were dozens of them, and the messages of 16 of them are included in the Bible. They were all very different. But, in different keys, tones, pitches and lengths, they all sang the same basic song.

In this study, we're going to focus on the message of Amos, a man from Judah who spoke God's words to Israel in around 750BC…

> **Read Amos 8 v 4-14**

2. How does Israel treat obedience to God's laws, such as resting on the Sabbath (v 5)?

• How do those with more wealth treat those with less?

3. Sum up what God tells Israel he will do:
    • verse 10:

    • verses 11-12:

    • verse 14:

4. What will be the sign that "that day" of God's judgment has arrived (v 9)?

Amos' song to Israel, part one: *Judgment is coming…*

➔ apply

5. How might the attitudes shown in 8 v 4-6 look in your church and your life today?

• What would the opposite (ie: true godliness) look like?

↓ investigate

❯ Read Amos 9 v 11-15

6. What will God do to David's fallen kingdom "in that day" (v 11)?

• Where will this kingdom stretch to?

• What will life be like for God's people (v 13-15)?

Amos' song to Israel, part two: ...*Salvation will follow.*

Three decades after Amos' message, Israel was invaded by Assyria, and the people taken into exile. Judah limped on for another century, before it too was obliterated, its people exiled to Babylon. There were few of them, far from the land, and without God's blessing. Judgment had come.

Yet two generations later, a few were able to return to the land to rebuild their homes. Salvation had followed. But the full promise of Amos 9 v 11-15, and of the whole of the Old Testament, remained unfulfilled. The people were few. They had no king. They did not experience the blessing of a life of plenty in God's land. And they kept on sinning. The Old Testament finishes with the people still facing judgment for sin, and still waiting for God to bring them the future he'd promised.

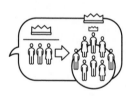

SNAPSHOT: 1 Kings 12 – Malachi

God's prophets warn his sinful people that judgment will come... but that salvation will follow. In the exile, the people have to leave the land. They return—but are still waiting for the amazing future beyond judgment that God has promised.

...*He has fulfilled*

⊕ investigate

▶ Read Luke 23 v 38-46

7. Why is the mocking sign above Jesus' head both ironic and tragic?

8. How does Amos' prophecy help us grasp what's happening in v 44-45a?

"The curtain of the temple" was a foot thick and stopped people going into the part of the temple where the perfect God was particularly present among his people. It was a constant visual reminder that sinful humans, including the Jews, could not live in the presence of God, enjoying his blessing.

9. Look at verse 45. What does this show Jesus' death has achieved?

In this section we see exactly what all this means for individuals, too.

10. What does the second criminal dying next to Jesus recognise about him, and ask him to do (v 40-42)?

• What does Jesus promise him about his future?

• How can someone experience the ultimate fulfilment of God's promises in the prophets, such as Amos 9 v 11-15?

⮕ apply

11. Imagine that someone had (for some reason!) read Amos 8 – 9, and wanted to know what it all means for us today. How would you explain to them what Amos tells us about…

• what the Lord Jesus' death saves people *from*?

• what the Lord Jesus' death saves people *for*?

12. What should we be looking forward to *most*? If we do, how will it affect our feelings and actions *now*?

⊡ getting personal

How often do you consider the future that Christ's cross has given you? How excited are you at that prospect?

What practical things can you put in place to make sure that the future the Lord won at the cross is something which dominates your thoughts, emotions and decisions each day?

⬆ pray

Thank God for...

Confess to God that...

Ask God for His help with...

⊡ explore more

▶ Read 2 Kings 17 v 1-13, 18-20

What happened (v 3-6)?

That's the human, political perspective—what was going on "under the surface" (v 18-20)?

Why (v 7-9a)?

How is what is happening here the opposite of God's promises
• to Abraham of people, land and blessing?
• to David, of a king who would rule under God, and for ever?
• in Amos 9 v 11-15?

How does this section underline how awful it is to face God's judgment?

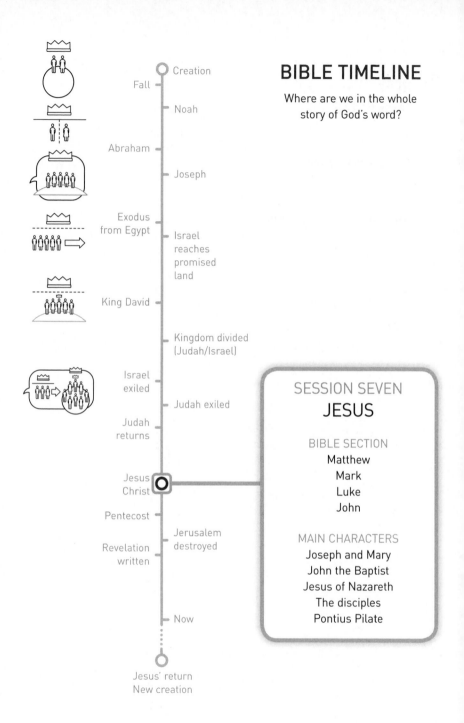

BIBLE TIMELINE

Where are we in the whole story of God's word?

Creation
Fall
Noah
Abraham
Joseph
Exodus from Egypt
Israel reaches promised land
King David
Kingdom divided (Judah/Israel)
Israel exiled
Judah exiled
Judah returns
Jesus Christ
Pentecost
Revelation written
Jerusalem destroyed
Now
Jesus' return
New creation

SESSION SEVEN
JESUS

BIBLE SECTION
Matthew
Mark
Luke
John

MAIN CHARACTERS
Joseph and Mary
John the Baptist
Jesus of Nazareth
The disciples
Pontius Pilate

7 Luke 9, 24
GOD IN HIS WORLD

JESUS OF NAZARETH

The story so far

The prophets warned God's disobedient people that judgment was coming—but also promised that salvation would follow. God judged his people by exiling them from his land. They have returned, but are still waiting for him to fulfil his promises.

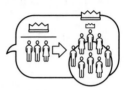

⊕ talkabout

1. In this session, we (finally!) reach the New Testament. What promises has God made through the Old Testament?

⊥ investigate

What we've missed: After Malachi, the last Old Testament prophet, God's people heard nothing from God for 400 years. In that time, the land was conquered by the Romans.

Then, in about 30AD, a new prophet arrived. His name was John. Lots of people wondered if he might be the Messiah, the one who'd fulfil all God's promises. But he said: "One who is more powerful than I will come, the straps of whose sandals I am not worthy to untie" (Luke 3 v 16). John wasn't the Messiah, but he'd been sent by God to announce that the Messiah was on his way…

▶ Read Luke 9 v 18-22

2.   What are the options as to who Jesus is (v 19-20)?

3.   Have a look at these passages and think about...
• How they suggest that Peter's verdict is the correct one.
• How they show Jesus fulfilling a promise of God.

• Luke 4 v 33-37:

• Luke 5 v 12-16:

• Luke 5 v 17-26:

• Luke 7 v 1-10:

• Luke 7 v 11-17:

• Luke 8 v 22-25:

Jesus doesn't disagree with Peter! But in 9 v 21, he does warn his friends not to talk about his identity, because first he wants to explain to them what will happen next...

4.   What four things does Jesus promise will happen to him (v 22)?

•

•

•

•

• Imagine you were a friend of Jesus the Messiah, listening to his words. You know what God has promised he will do through his ever-ruling King. How would you feel about what Jesus says here?

5. **Read Luke 9 v 23-26.** How is the life that the Messiah's followers will experience similar to Jesus' own?

• What promise does Jesus make (v 24)?

→ apply

6. What would the world around you make of verse 24? Why?

• When do we find it hardest to live by verse 24? Why?

⊌ investigate

Jesus' prediction began to come true. He was arrested, tried, mocked and beaten, rejected and killed. But you don't need to be God's Messiah to predict you will die—or even to say how you'll die! To predict your own resurrection, on the other hand…

▶ Read Luke 24 v 1-12, 36-49

7. Jesus has been buried, but is tomb is empty. Why, according to the angels (v 5-6)?

8. Pick out the things that happen in these two passages which give us confidence that Jesus had really risen from the dead.

9. Why should the women at the tomb have known Jesus would rise (v 6-7)?

• Why should the men in the room have known he would rise (v 44, 46)?

10. What does Jesus promise his followers is now available (v 47, 49)?

→ **apply**

11. What does the resurrection prove about...
  • Jesus' identity?

  • Jesus' words?

  • Jesus' promises?

12. How should Jesus' resurrection from the dead change the way we look at our lives now, and our lives in the future?

SNAPSHOT: Matthew – John

Jesus is the One who fulfils all God's Old Testament promises. He calls people to live under his loving rule, and brings God's blessing to those who follow him. He has defeated the devil, death and sin. And he has risen from the dead to prove he is the Messiah and to offer a future beyond judgment.

getting personal

A true follower of Jesus, who knows that he is the risen fulfilment of all God's promises, is willing to "lose" their life—to give up anything in order to follow him.

Can you point to ways in which you have done, or are doing, this?

Where are you failing to? How will these two facts help you to start carrying your cross:

- Jesus died on his cross not just as your example, but in your place, for all the times you don't live his way.
- Jesus rose from the dead on a particular day in history, to prove that he is the One who can make all God's promises true for you.

pray

Read 2 Corinthians 1 v 20.

Each take a minute to choose a particular promise of God which especially excites you today. Then spend time **thanking God** that those promises have been made "Yes" for you in Jesus.

Tell God how you are struggling to deny yourself to follow his Messiah. Ask him to change you so that you'll give up what you want in order to live how Jesus wants in that area.

⊡ explore more

optional

Jesus said he would be "rejected by the elders, the chief priests and the teachers of the law" (Luke 9 v 22)—in other words, the leaders of Israel, the people who were supposed to love and obey God. God's Messiah ended up being put to death in Jerusalem, the capital city of God's ancient people.

And Jesus told a story, a parable, which explained what Israel was doing, and what God would do in response.

> **Read Luke 20 v 9-19**

The vineyard is Israel; the tenants are the Jews; and the owner is God.

What has God asked for; and how has Israel responded (v 9-12)?

What awful decision does Israel then make (v 13-15)?

What will God do next (v 16)?

Jesus' crucifixion is what's being talked about in verse 15. What should we expect to see happening next (v 16)?

How is this story both a warning and an exciting promise?

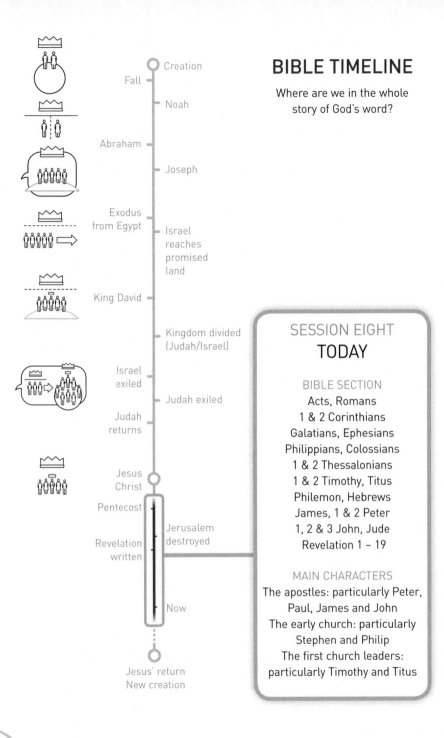

BIBLE TIMELINE

Where are we in the whole story of God's word?

Creation
Fall
Noah
Abraham
Joseph
Exodus from Egypt
Israel reaches promised land
King David
Kingdom divided (Judah/Israel)
Israel exiled
Judah exiled
Judah returns
Jesus Christ
Pentecost
Revelation written
Jerusalem destroyed
Now
Jesus' return
New creation

SESSION EIGHT
TODAY

BIBLE SECTION
Acts, Romans
1 & 2 Corinthians
Galatians, Ephesians
Philippians, Colossians
1 & 2 Thessalonians
1 & 2 Timothy, Titus
Philemon, Hebrews
James, 1 & 2 Peter
1, 2 & 3 John, Jude
Revelation 1 – 19

MAIN CHARACTERS
The apostles: particularly Peter, Paul, James and John
The early church: particularly Stephen and Philip
The first church leaders: particularly Timothy and Titus

8 Acts 1 – 2
HEAR THE MESSAGE

TODAY

The story so far

Jesus is the One who fulfils all God's Old Testament promises. He calls people to live under his loving rule, enjoying God's blessing. He has defeated the devil, death and sin. And he has risen from the dead to prove he is the Messiah and to offer a future beyond judgment.

⊕ talkabout

1. Being in heaven is better than being in this present world. All Christ's followers will have life in heaven. So why do you think God doesn't take Christians to heaven now?!

⊕ investigate

At the end of Luke's Gospel, we left the risen Jesus speaking to his followers, promising them the Holy Spirit—"power from on high" (Luke 24 v 49). Luke wrote a second volume, which we call Acts. If the subtitle to Luke's Gospel could be: "What Jesus did on earth", then Acts would be subtitled: "What Jesus did next".

❯ Read Acts 1 v 7-11

2. Jesus is speaking in verses 7-8. Circle on the map over the page the areas he mentions in verse 8.

3. Imagine you are one of the handful of followers Jesus has at this point. How would you feel about the prospect of obeying the second half of verse 8, do you think?!

• Why would the first half of verse 8 be a great comfort to you?

In verse 9, Jesus goes back into his Father's presence (which the cloud is a sign of, see Luke 9 v 34-35 and Session Five).

4. What do the "men dressed in white" say is the next major event in God's plan, following the "ascension"?

> **Read Acts 2 v 1-15, 22-24, 37-41**

5. In verses 1-4, the Holy Spirit comes to these Christians. What do these verses tell us about who he is, and what he does?

6. How does the Spirit-filled Peter start doing what Jesus had asked in 1 v 8?

• How do people respond to these Spirit-filled Christians?

• v 12:

• v 13:

• v 41:

⮕ apply

7. What are Jesus' followers on earth to do today?

• How does Acts 1 v 8 encourage us to get on with doing this?

8. How have you seen the three responses to the Christians in Acts 2 in your Christian life? Does the fact that we see them here encourage or challenge you, or both? Why?

⊡ getting personal

What counts as a "good day" for you? A day where you have devoted yourself to your church family? Where you have told someone else about Jesus the Messiah, his life, death and resurrection —even if they've laughed at you?

Being part of God's mission to his world is exciting, and eternally significant—it can also seem daunting. How wonderful that we can ask the Spirit to give us the priorities and courage we don't naturally have!

⊡ investigate

> **Read Acts 2 v 42-47**

9. This is the first Christian church. What do we see here about what church is, and what church does?

• What is challenging about the word "devoted" in verse 42?

10. What does verse 47 tell us about the way the Lord works through his people? Why is this exciting?

11. So far, we've seen God's Spirit-filled people witnessing about his Son in Jerusalem. Read these parts of Acts and use the map on page 60 to trace the progress of the message about Jesus: 8 v 1b-8; 11 v 19-21; 17 v 13-15, 32-34; 28 v 11-16, 30-31.

• How does Acts show God's people obeying his mission command in 1 v 8? How does Acts show God's promise to Abram being fulfilled?

⊡ apply

12. What have we seen about the priorities Christians should have between Jesus' ascension and his return?

• What can make it hard to have these priorities? How do Acts 1 and 2 help us and encourage us in our task?

SNAPSHOT: Acts – Revelation 19

God has sent his Spirit to live in his Son's followers, enabling them to tell people about his Son. His church has spread from Jerusalem to Rome and beyond. The mission of God's people today is to be devoted to each other and to witness about his Son throughout his world.

getting personal

It must have been wonderful to have been part of the Acts 2 church! All too often, our churches fall far short of that one.

Let's not make the mistake of thinking our churches…
• could never be like that, or
• would be like that if only others would be more committed.

Our churches will change and grow as *we* become more devoted to them. So what practical things could *you* start doing, or do more of, out of devotion to your Christian community?

pray

Thank God for giving you a place in his mission to have the whole world hear the message about Jesus the Messiah, and for the power of his Spirit to enable you to do your part. Thank God for giving you a church community to be devoted to.

Share the names of some people you would like to tell about Jesus. Why not commit to praying for each other for the next year? **Ask God** to give each of you opportunities to talk about his Son, and the courage to take them.

optional

⊡ explore more

We've seen that the Spirit lives in Christians to help us change the world by talking to people about Jesus the Messiah. But he dwells in us to change *us*, too.

❯ Read Galatians 5 v 16-25

Paul is writing to a church in modern-day Turkey.

What fight is going on inside every Christian (v 17)?

What kind of things are examples of a lifestyle which is rebelling against King Jesus (v 19-21)?

What does Jesus' Spirit work to replace those things with (v 22-24)?

How should Christ's followers try to live (v 16, 25)?

How do these verses challenge you? How do they encourage you?

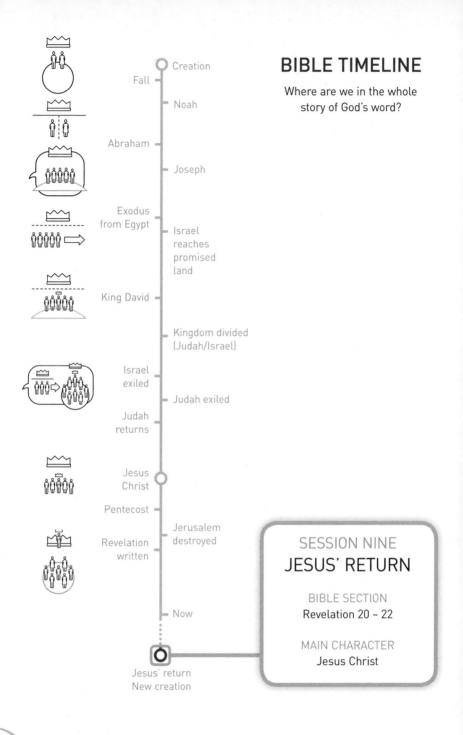

BIBLE TIMELINE

Where are we in the whole
story of God's word?

Creation
Fall
Noah
Abraham
Joseph
Exodus
from Egypt
Israel
reaches
promised
land
King David
Kingdom divided
(Judah/Israel)
Israel
exiled
Judah exiled
Judah
returns
Jesus
Christ
Pentecost
Jerusalem
destroyed
Revelation
written
Now
Jesus' return
New creation

SESSION NINE
JESUS' RETURN

BIBLE SECTION
Revelation 20 – 22

MAIN CHARACTER
Jesus Christ

9

Revelation 20 – 22
IN A PERFECT WORLD

JESUS' RETURN

The story so far

God's Spirit lives in his people, enabling them to tell other people about Jesus' life, death and resurrection. The mission of God's people today is to be devoted to each other and to tell people the truth about his Son throughout his world.

⊕ talkabout

1. For this world to become perfect, what would have to change? What would have to go?

⊥ investigate

The Bible's last book, Revelation, is a vision given to the apostle John. It's a fascinating, strange and exhilarating book, and Christians don't always agree about every detail in it! Most of it describes what the world is like now, from heaven's perspective. In chapter 20, the focus shifts to what the world will be like when its Creator returns—the final act in God's plan.

❯ Read Revelation 20 v 11 – 21 v 5

2. What is at the centre of this scene (20 v 11, 21 v 5)?

3. What will God shut out of his world? Why is each of these "evictions" necessary if his world is to be made perfect?
  • 20 v 14:

  • 20 v 12, 15, look on to 21 v 8:

  • Look back to 20 v 10:

  • 21 v 4:

4. Re-read 21 v 2-7. How is this future event the complete fulfilment of God's promises…
  • that creation will be "very good" (Genesis 1 v 31)?

  • to Adam and Eve, of someone to crush the devil and conquer sin and death (Genesis 3 v 15)?

  • to Abraham, of a people in a land enjoying God's blessing (Genesis 12 v 1-3)?

  • to David, of an everlasting, perfect ruler (2 Samuel 7)?

• to the prophets, of a wonderful future beyond judgment (eg: Amos 9 v 11-15)?

Who will live in this perfect, amazing world? We will all be "judged according to what [we have] done" (20 v 12). And what we have all done is to sin. So our place should be in the "lake of fire" (v 15).

5. What does verse 15 suggest is the only way out of this eternal misery?

• **Read 13 v 8; 21 v 27.** This book belongs to "the Lamb who was slain"—to Jesus. How is this the ultimate fulfilment of God's promise to Moses (which we saw in Session Four)?

☐ apply

6. 21 v 7 promises: "Those who are victorious will inherit all this"—or, as the NIV84 translates it: "He who overcomes will inherit all this. Life as a follower of the crucified, risen Jesus before his return is hard. How can we use Revelation 20 – 21 to encourage each other to keep going?

⊌ investigate

❯ Read Revelation 22 v 1-5

7. Compare this future eternal city to God's original garden creation. How is it similar? How is it even better?

Garden in Genesis	City in Revelation
2 v 9	22 v 1-2
3 v 8a, 2 v 15-16	22 v 4a
1 v 26-28	22 v 3b, 5b
1 v 14-16	22 v 5

• How does this make you feel?

SNAPSHOT: Revelation 20 – 22

When he returns, Jesus will judge and punish all that is wrong with the world, including sin, death and the devil. He will recreate the world perfectly, and live with his perfect people as their King in this perfect, eternal place.

It's going to be amazing!

⊍ investigate

8. The last word of Revelation, and therefore the Bible, means "This is true". **Read Revelation 1 v 12-19.** This is the beginning of John's vision. How does it give us certainty that what he has written down is true?

⊝ apply

9. What is one right response to knowing this is the future (22 v 20b)? What difference will saying and meaning this make to life now?

10. Can you remember: the title of each session (they're alphabetised!)?

A	**B**
C	**D**
E	**F**
G	**H**
I	

• the promises made in Sessions 1 – 6?

• how Jesus is the way God keeps each promise?

⊡ getting personal

If you are a follower of the Lamb, Revelation 21 – 22 is your future. How often do you think about where you are headed as a Christian?

Next time you have a difficult or painful day, how are you going to remind yourself of where you will be one future day? Will you let it make a difference to your emotions and your actions?

⊡ pray

Spend time giving thanks for who Jesus is, and then for the future he has given his people.

Share things which tend to stop you remembering and being joyful about where you're headed, and then pray for one another.

⊡ explore more

optional

▶ **Read 2 Peter 3 v 2-14**

What will happen between Jesus' ascension and return (v 3-6)?

How does Peter answer these "scoffers" (v 8, 10)?

Why has the Lord not yet fulfilled his promise to return (v 9)?

What should the Lord Jesus Christ's followers do until he returns?
• *v 2*
• *v 11-13*
• *v 14*

Promises kept

The whole story of the Bible

LEADER'S GUIDE

Leader's Guide

INTRODUCTION

Leading a Bible study can be a bit like herding cats—everyone has a different idea of what the passage could be about, and a different line of enquiry that they want to pursue. But a good group leader is more than someone who just referees this kind of discussion. You will want to:

• correctly understand and handle the Bible passage. But also...

• encourage and train the people in your group to do this for themselves. Don't fall into the trap of spoon-feeding people by simply passing on the information in the Leader's Guide. Then...

• make sure that no Bible study is finished without everyone knowing how the passage is relevant for them. What changes do you all need to make in the light of the things you have been learning? And finally...

• encourage the group to turn all that has been learned and discussed into prayer.

Your Bible-study group is unique, and you are likely to know better than anyone the capabilities, backgrounds and circumstances of the people you are leading. That's why we've designed these guides with a number of optional features. If they're a quiet bunch, you might want to spend longer on talkabout. If your time is limited, you can choose to skip explore more, or get people to look at these questions at home. Can't get enough of Bible study? Well, some studies have optional extra homework projects. As leader, you can adapt and select the material to the needs of your particular group.

So what's in the Leader's Guide? The main thing that this Leader's Guide will help you to do is to understand the major teaching points in the passage you are studying, and how to apply them. As well as guidance on the questions, the Leader's Guide for each session contains the following important sections:

THE BIG IDEA

One key sentence will give you the main point of the session. This is what you should be aiming to have fixed in people's minds as they leave the Bible study. And it's the point you need to head back towards when the discussion goes off at a tangent.

SUMMARY

An overview of the passage, including plenty of useful historical background information.

OPTIONAL EXTRA

Usually this is an introductory activity that aims to introduce the main theme of the study (and to "break the ice" at the beginning of the session), or it can be used later to reinforce the teaching points. Optional Extra doesn't appear in every single study in this Good Book Guide.

Let's take a look at the various different features of a study:

⊕ talkabout

Each session kicks off with a discussion question, based on the group's opinions or experiences. It's designed to get people talking and thinking in a general way about the main subject of the Bible study.

⬇ investigate

The first thing you and your group need to know is what the Bible passage is about, which is the purpose of these questions. But watch out—people may come up with answers based on their experiences or teaching they have heard in the past, without referring to the passage at all. It's amazing how often we can get through a Bible study without actually looking at the Bible! If you're stuck for an answer, the Leader's Guide contains guidance on questions. These are the answers to direct your group to. This information isn't meant to be read out to people—ideally, you want them to discover these answers from the Bible for themselves. Sometimes there are optional follow-up questions (see ☑ in Guidance on Questions) to help you help your group get to the answer.

⋮⋮ explore more

These questions generally point people to other relevant parts of the Bible. They are useful for helping your group to see how the passage fits into the "big picture" of the whole Bible. These sections are OPTIONAL—only use them if you have time. Remember that it's better to finish in good time having really grasped one big thing from the passage, than to try and cram everything in.

➔ apply

We want to encourage you to spend more time working at application—too often, it is simply tacked on at the end. In the Good Book Guides, apply sections are mixed in with the investigate sections of the study. We hope that people will realise that application is not just an optional extra, but rather, the whole purpose of studying the

Bible. We do Bible study so that our lives can be changed by what we hear from God's word. If you skip the application, the Bible study hasn't achieved its purpose.

These questions draw out practical lessons that we can all learn from the Bible passage. You can review what has been learned so far, and think about practical differences that this should make in our churches and our lives. The group gets the opportunity to talk about what they personally have learned.

⬇ getting personal

These can be done at home, but it is well worth allowing a few moments of quiet reflection during the study for each person to think and pray about specific changes they need to make in their own lives. Why not have a time for reporting back at the beginning of the following session, so that everyone can be encouraged and challenged by one another to make application a priority?

⬆ pray

In Acts 4 v 25-30 the first Christians quoted Psalm 2 as they prayed in response to the persecution of the apostles by the Jewish religious leaders. Today however, it's not as common for Christians to base prayers on the truths of God's word as it once was. As a result, our prayers tend to be weak, superficial and self-centred rather than bold, visionary and God-centred.

The prayer section is based on what has been learned from the Bible passage. How different our prayer times would be if we were genuinely responding to what God has said to us through his word.

Promises Kept: Special Features

This particular Good Book Guide has a few elements which don't appear in the rest of the range.

PROMISES FULFILLED

Studies One – Six are each in two parts:
What God has promised... You'll look at an Old Testament passage, seeing what happened in that period of history, and a promise God made.
...he has fulfilled: The study moves to a section of a Gospel, to see an aspect of how Jesus is the One who keeps that particular promise of God.

SNAPSHOT

Each session includes a "snapshot", which sums up what has happened in the period of history you're looking at. The Leader's Guide will explain what they show, but the key below will also help:

——————— No relationship

— — — — Imperfect relationship

◯ Perfect

◯ Good, but not perfect

▭ A future that's been promised

TIMELINES

Most Good Book Guides start with a timeline, but this one has one at the beginning of each session. You can use them to recap on what you've already seen in previous sessions (the snapshots are included down the left-hand side) and to see the point in history the study will focus on. Each timeline page also tells you what Bible books cover all or part of the period you're looking at, and who the "famous" biblical characters in that period are. Where necessary, the page includes a map showing you where the action is taking place.

EXPLORE MORE

These come at the end of each session. Unless indicated in the Leader's Guide, they pick up on a part of the Bible that lies between the session and the next one. Each session is pretty full anyway, so don't feel under any pressure to use Explore More!

SOME TIPS

In most of the sessions in this Good Book Guide, you'll be covering huge chunks of time, and big chunks of the Bible narrative. So two key things to remember are:

Keep on course! Your group will probably ask lots of questions about lots of things which are in the Bible book you're in, or which happened in the historical period you're covering. But the session isn't trying to unpack everything in the passage, the book or the period—don't let questions knock you off course! Encourage your group to keep on track, and to ask questions about what you are talking about, rather than what you aren't.

Keep it simple! There are lots of important Bible themes this guide doesn't pick up on. For instance, neither covenant nor temple are mentioned much at all. That's because if we aim to do too much, we end up doing nothing in a way that people can grasp, apply and remember. Don't give in to the temptation to add complications!

1
Genesis 1; John 1
A VERY GOOD WORLD

THE BIG IDEA

God is Creator: humans are his creatures, made in his image, to rule his very good world under him. In the coming of Jesus, God is beginning a new creation.

SUMMARY

The Bible begins "in the beginning" of what we call history. The first sentence of the Bible gives the biblical worldview—that God is eternal, and that he created everything (physical and spiritual). God is therefore the ruler of all things—and humans are his creatures, made by him. And, uniquely in all creation, we are made in God's image (Genesis 1 v 28). We are made to relate to him as he speaks to us; and to reflect back to creation his character and his loving rule.

The "promise" in Genesis 1 is not explicit; but we do see that God's purpose is for his people to enjoy living in his perfect world under his loving rule, ie: "rest" (2 v 2). This is what he calls "very good" (1 v 31). And it should prompt us to wonder, as we look around at our less-than-perfect world, whether God's plans have been thwarted.

Which is why the start of John's Gospel, where this session finishes, is such good news. John 1 deliberately echoes Genesis 1; and we discover that the Word, God, walked in his creation as a man, Jesus (v 17). The Word came to bring "light", which is "life" (v 4). John wants us to see that in Jesus, the Word made flesh, God is beginning to recreate his world perfectly.

GUIDANCE ON QUESTIONS

1. What is the most naturally beautiful or spectacular part of the world you've seen? How did visiting it make you feel? Some may have visited exotic locations; others may talk about something closer to home. And the feelings will be varied: awe, wonder, thankfulness, gratitude, humility.

2. What did God do (v 1)? Made everything. Don't allow your group to get sidetracked about where (and if) the "Big Bang" or other scientific theories fit in. Genesis isn't really interested in that; it wants us to grasp something theological, not scientific—that God is the Creator of all.

• **How did he do it (v 3)? What does this show us about what he is like?** Through speaking. God is all-powerful—it required no huge effort for him to create light. He simply spoke, and it happened! God creates through his word (this will be important later on in the study, for Q9-11).

Note: Your group may ask about the way Genesis "fits" with modern scientific discoveries and theories, and this would be a good place to point out that we shouldn't approach Genesis as though it is a scientific manual. For a helpful and short video answer on this issue, go to: www.christianityexplored.org/tough-questions/scienceandchristianity

3. Split into pairs or small groups. Pick two or three of these sections each to have a look at: Genesis 1 v 6-8, 9-13, 14-19, 20-23. • What is happening in each of the sections you've looked at?
1 v 6-8: God separates water above from below—"sky".
1 v 9-13: God creates land and seas... God creates plant life on the land.

1 v 14-19: God creates sun, moon and stars, making the day light and the night dark (notice v 16—"He also made the stars"—trillions of them, just with a word!)

1 v 20-23: God creates fish to live in the sea, and birds to fly through the air.

- **What similarities do you see between them?**
  - God is creating.
  - God creates through his powerful word.
  - It happens just as God says (notice the "and it was so", v 7, 9, 11, 15).
  - Time passes in each section—each is a "day" (Christians differ over whether we are to understand this as a 24-hour period each time, or as an "era").
  - *Days One and Two:* God names what he's created (v 5, 8).
  - *Days Three – Five:* "God saw that it was good" (v 10, 12, 18, 21).
  - *Days Three and Five:* God makes plants, fish and birds "according to their kinds" (v 12, 21). There is a purpose to, and an order in, creation.
  - Each part of creation has a point, a purpose to serve. No part is useless, wasted or valueless.

4. What have we learned about God?
Talk about what's particularly struck your group, but key points are:
- God is the creator.
- God is all-powerful.
- God creates through his word.
- God creates order, and what is "good".

5. What was the last thing God made (v 26-28)? Mankind, male and female.

- **What is different about how this part of his creation is described? What does this mean, do you think?** Mankind is the only part of creation God makes "in

his own image" (v 27). That's so crucial it's repeated twice (v 26, 27). There are various aspects to what this means:
(1) An image of something is like the "original", though not identical. Mankind represents God on earth, and shows something of God to the rest of creation (including each other). Verse 28 suggests that we are like God in our ability and impulse to rule creation.
(2) God doesn't only speak *about* humanity (v 26), he also speaks *to* humanity (v 28). Because we bear God's image, humanity has a unique relationship with God. We can know and hear him.
(3) Humanity is unique among creation. We have some similarities to the animal kingdom—but we are not simply animals. We are God's image-bearers—with great value, and great responsibility.

- **What job does God give them (v 28)?**
To rule his creation, and to fill the earth by increasing in number (one God-given job that humanity has actually managed!) "Subdue" here doesn't mean "oppress", but to "manage". Just as God rules his creation lovingly and for its own good, so he gives mankind the task of ruling it lovingly under him.

⊻

- **What action is the first one used in the description of God's relationship with people (v 28)? What does this mean?** "Blessed". This means to enjoy life in God's world, under his loving rule.

6. What is God's verdict on His creation (v 31)? "Very good". God is totally pleased.

7. APPLY: How does humanity's place in creation…
- **make us humble?** We are not God. We

are not ultimately in charge. We depend on Another for everything.

- **make us valuable?** We are, uniquely, made in God's image, to relate to him and to reflect his image.

- **give us purpose in life?** God has put us here to know him, and look after his creation (including other people).

8. There are many issues in society today where knowing we are creatures, made in God's image, to rule his world, should shape our view. Pick a few now, and discuss what Gen 1 v 26-31 has to say about them. Your group will come up with what particularly concerns them, so allow them to shape the discussion (as long as you feel Genesis 1 v 26-31 has something to say about that issue!) Encourage people to use v 26-31, not just their own views. *Some ideas:*

- *The beginning and end of life.* Since God created life, and we are made in his image, each life has intrinsic value. We are not God, so should not presume to end a life simply because it is unwanted, be that our life or someone else's. So these verses help shape a Christian response to both abortion and euthanasia. **Note:** Remember that there may be those in your group who this is a very sensitive issue for.

- *The environment.* God has given us the job of ruling this world, and we should do so in a sustainable way. We are not simply to exploit the world's resources without doing so responsibly. Equally, we are to rule. When some argue that humanity should just get out of the way, that we are the problem, they are half right—but humanity must also be the solution.

- *Atheism and secularism.* If our core identity is as image-bearing creatures, we must resist attempts to make ourselves God.

Without God, things don't make sense.

- *Science.* Not everything can be explained by science—true scientific experimentation is seeking to discover the *How* and *When*, but not the *Who* or the *Why*. Science can't tell us who we are, whether and why we have value, or why we are here.

SNAPSHOT

The crown represents God, and the figures the people he's made to enjoy his world, living in it and ruling it under him.

9. What similarities are there between these verses and Genesis 1 v 1-5?
- Both start "in the beginning".
- Both mention God, and his Word.
- Both talk about creation.
- Both speak about light.

At the beginning of his Gospel about Jesus, John deliberately uses creation-ish language.

10. What do we learn about "the Word"?
- **v 1:** He was with God from eternity—in fact he is God.
- **v 2:** The Word is eternal.
- **v 3:** Everything was made through "the Word". Here, he is seen to be a person.
- **v 4:** The Word gives life.
- **v 5:** The life (or "light") that the Word gives is misunderstood by those who are without it ("darkness").

11. Read verse 14. What is amazing about these words? The eternal, creating, powerful Word became a human being.

God stepped into his creation as a creature. At a particular point in history, it was possible to see God, the One who came from the Father's side and lived on earth.

- **God's word brought light to creation (Genesis 1 v 5)—here, the Word became flesh to bring "light", too. What is that "light" (John 1 v 4)?** "Life". The "light" that God became human to bring was life.

- **This Word was called Jesus (v 17) … How is God "creating" through Jesus coming to earth?** By bringing life.

If your group is struggling with this question, you might like to ask these questions to help them to the answer:
- What have we seen is being echoed in John 1? Genesis 1—God's creation.
- How did God create, and bring life, in Genesis 1? Through his Word.
- What has come to earth at the start of John's Gospel (v14)? his Word.
- What should we expect to see God's Word doing, that John's alerted us to in the way he's begun his Gospel? Creating, and bringing life.

EXPLORE MORE: Genesis 2 v 18-25
What is "not good"? That the man is alone (2 v 18).
What does God do about it (v 20b-22)? He makes a "helper" for him—a woman.
Note: The word helper is not a negative description. God is sometimes described as a "helper" (eg: Deuteronomy 33 v 29; Psalm 118 v 7). Men and women are different, yet equally bear the image of God.
What relationship have they been made for (v 24)? Marriage (see Mark 10 v 5-12, where Genesis 2 v 24 is linked with marriage in v 11-12). Sex is the physical expression this committed relationship.
What kind of relationship do they enjoy in God's very good world (v 25)? A very trusting, intimate one. They're able to be completely vulnerable in front of each other, without shame or worry.
What do these verses tell us about men and women? Men and women are equally valuable, made by God, and yet different, made to "go with" one another. God made us to enjoy the intimacy, trust and joy of a committed, lifelong, sexual relationship (marriage).

Genesis 3; Luke 11

2 BROKEN BY REBELLION

BIG IDEA
Humanity listened to the devil and rejected God's rule. So we now face imperfect life and then death. Jesus came to defeat the power of the devil, as God has promised.

SUMMARY
Genesis 3 marks the most catastrophic moment in history—"the fall". Instead of enjoying the blessing of life under God's perfect rule, the first humans chose to listen to the devil (the "snake", or the "serpent"), and rejected God as their ruling, life-giving God. Every single human has done this ever since—all of us sin (Romans 3 v 23).

This brings God's judgment. Judgment

impacts their relationship with the world, each other and God. Humans now face the spiritual death of life without God, followed by physical death (Genesis 3 v 17-19).

Their bid for independence from God leaves them under the tyranny of the devil. He is able to point to humans' rebellion against God and so insist that God judges them, because God is perfectly just. The devil's weapon against us is our sin—his great triumph over us is our death.

But God promises that there will come a descendant of the woman who will break the devil's power (ie: his ability to point to our sin, so that we must die). In Luke 11, we find that this descendant is Jesus—he has the power to break the devil's hold over us, to tie him up, and to carry off his spoils ie: us (v 22). Jesus has come to defeat the devil, in fulfilment of the promise of Genesis 3 v 15, and he has the power to do so.

GUIDANCE FOR QUESTIONS

1. As you look at the world today, in what ways is it still "very good"? In what ways isn't it? Your group will be able to give some aspects of creation that are still "very good" (Genesis 1 v 31)—natural beauty, the times when people are good to one another, the gift of a newborn baby, fulfilling work—and some that certainly are not "very good"—wars, illnesses, death.

- **What reasons do people give for the world and people not being "very good"?** Some possibilities:
  - This is just the world that happened to be made by blind random chance, and so it's just how it is.
  - Because humans get corrupted by society and authority, and so don't work together. If they did, it would be fine.
  - Because humans don't act rationally. If we all thought things through and lived

according to our reason (however that's defined), things would be better.
- Actually, this is a very good world, and people are basically good. We shouldn't be so negative about life!
- Then of course there's the biblical answer: humanity have rejected God's rule, and so come under his judgment. You don't need to mention it at this point if your group don't.

2. What do the woman and the man, who God had created, do? They listen to the serpent's persuasion (the woman) and to their spouse (the man), and eat the fruit from the tree God told them not to (v 3, 6).

- **Read Genesis 2 v 15-17. What is so serious about their actions?** God had warned them that they would "certainly die" if they did this.
  Note: "Knowledge" in v 17 carries the sense of "deciding". By eating from this tree, humanity said that they wanted the right to decide what was good and evil in the world—in other words, to rule the world themselves, rejecting God as the ruler who decides right and wrong.

3. What tactics does the snake—the devil—use as he tempts the woman?
- **v 1:** He encourages the woman to doubt what God said: "Did God really say…?"
- **v 4:** He prompts her to doubt God's words are true: "You will not certainly die…"
- **v 4:** He encourages her to doubt the goodness of God, to see God not as her loving ruler who wants what's best for her, but as a tyrant who is denying her what she needs. He promises her god-likeness.
  Note: Revelation 12 v 9 calls Satan "the snake"—so snake in Genesis 3 = devil.

4. What is it that convinces the woman and the man to disobey God (v 5-6)?

- The promise they can be "like God", ruling themselves instead of ruled by him (v 5).
- Their eyes and stomachs suggest it would be a good idea (v 6a). They're led by their feelings and physical desires.
- The hope of gaining wisdom (v 6a). This isn't godly wisdom—this is worldly wisdom, which ignores God and decides for itself what's right and wrong.
- In the man's case, he's convinced by the example of his wife (v 6b). He seems simply to follow her lead, rather than remembering what God had said.

⊻

- **In Genesis 1-2, we saw God's creation order was him as loving ruler, and man and woman ruling under him over creation, with the woman helping the man. How has all this been turned upside down?** Part of creation (the snake) has convinced the woman to do something, which the man follows ("helps") her in. God has been relegated to a role beneath humanity, who decide when they will/won't obey him.

5. APPLY: How do we experience the same tactics when the devil tempts us? Let your group discuss this, based on the four "convincers" the devil used with the first man and woman. You could discuss a particular common sin eg: lying, or gossip.

6. What effect does rejecting God and deciding to make the rules themselves have on the man and woman's...
- **relationship with each other (v 7, 16—look back at 2 v 25 to compare)?**
  v 7: They cover up from each other. They are no longer open with and trusting of each other.
  v 16: "Desire" means "want to control

and dominate" and "rule" has the idea of harshness. People now seek to manipulate, control and dominate each other. There's been no perfect marriage since Genesis 2.
- **relationship with God (v 8, 23)?**
  v 8: They hide from their Creator. They withdraw from their closeness to God.
  v 23: The Creator withdraws from them. He will not allow them to live in his presence, in relationship with him.
- **relationship with what God's created (v 16-18)?**
  v 16: Childbirth will now be painful. Part of the way in which humans fulfil God's command to fill the earth (1 v 28) will now be marked by suffering.
  v 17-18: Creation will not work perfectly for humans. Adam will still be able to get food from the ground, but it will be hard.
  Note: This is why creation does not work properly. It is part of God's judgment.
- **future (v 19, 24)?** Shut out from Eden and the tree of life (v 24), humans can no longer enjoy life, or enjoy life for ever. All human bodies die and become dust (v 19).

7. Think about what humans had been created to enjoy in God's creation. How are these verses a reversal of those things? The reversal is complete:
- Made to enjoy life in God's world, humans will now know pain and hardship.
- Made to rule a very good creation, now creation can't be controlled / subdued.
- Made to enjoy relationship with God, humans are banished from his presence.
- Made to enjoy each other, humans no longer know complete trust and openness.

8. Look at what God says to the snake in v 14-15. What promise does God make (v 15)? Eve's descendants and the devil's (presumably demons) will be enemies—humanity will never quite settle for the captivity of death. One day humanity will crush the devil, even as he inflicts damage on humans (or a human).

- **How does this give hope to humanity?** The power of the devil is not unlimited. He is also under God's judgment. At some point in human history, he and his power over humans—death—will be crushed.

SNAPSHOT
The solid line means a broken relationship, the dotted one an imperfect relationship. There is no very good world anymore.

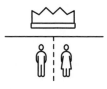

9. What is Jesus doing (Luke 11 v 14)? Driving out a demon from a man.

10. What answer does Jesus give (v 17-19)? Far from working for the devil, what does he say he has come to earth to do (v 20)? He points out it'd be ridiculous for the devil to undo his own work in the man! Jesus hasn't come to do the devil's work, but to be the way God re-establishes "the kingdom of God" (v 20) in a world under Satan's power, so people can live under his rule and enjoy his blessing.

- **… Who is the "strong man" of verse 21? Who is the "someone stronger" of verse 22?** The devil (we are his "possessions", facing death). Jesus (he will take the devil's possessions—people—as his "spoils", to live in his kingdom).

11. How is Jesus the fulfilment of the promise of Genesis 3 v 15? He is the one who can crush the devil. He is a human, but more powerful than Satan. Having never rejected God (see Luke 4 v 1-13; Hebrews 4 v 15—where Jesus is called "high priest"), he is uniquely able to defeat the devil. **Note:** You could say that Jesus ultimately does this on the cross, by dying in the place of sinners, removing the devil's power over us. But you might leave this until Session Six, and refer back to Genesis 3 v 15 then.

12. APPLY: From this session and the previous one, how would you explain to a friend… You could do this in pairs, alternating "explainer" and "friend" roles. Encourage people to make sure they are using the truths of Genesis 3 and Luke 11.

- **what our world is like and why?** Our world is beautiful, made by an amazing God. But it's also flawed, because we have rejected God's rule. Part of his judgment on us is that his world is no longer perfect.

- **what humans are like, and why?** We are amazing—wonderfully designed, capable of goodness and intelligence—because we are made in the image of God. But we are also deeply flawed—we don't treat others, ourselves, or the world around us as we should, even when we're trying to—because we're all, at heart, rebels against the God who made us.

- **how the problems of the world and humanity can be fixed?** No human or society which has rejected God (ie: everyone!) can hope to fix the problem of rejecting God, of being under the devil's power, of facing death. Only the sinless human, Jesus, can do that.

EXPLORE MORE: Genesis 11 v 1-9 What do people decide to do, and why (Gen 11 v 1-4)? Build a city. It will have "a tower that reaches to the heavens" (v 4) to show how powerful and independent they are—to "make a name for ourselves" (v 4). They do this to not be "scattered" (v 4).

God had told humanity to "fill the earth" (1 v 28) What do these people think of God's plan (v 4)? They are ignoring God's plans for his creation.

What ends up happening, and why (v 7-9)? God confuses their languages (v 7). They stop building, and are scattered (v 8)—exactly what they'd hoped to avoid!

How is this historical episode similar to what happened in Genesis 3? Humans decide to rule without reference to God, rejecting his plans for creation (notice the people don't mention God at all in v 1-4). But it's futile: God sees, and judges.

What are we seeing about what God is like? And about what humans are like? God sees, is in control, and judges. And his plans will happen. People are rebels against God. What we saw on a personal level in Gen 3 here happens with a whole society.

---

3 Genesis 12, 21; John 8
COVENANT MADE

THE BIG IDEA
God promised Abram people, land and blessing, and that one of his descendants would bring blessing to all peoples. Abram responded to God's promises by trusting in them, and showed this by obeying God.

SUMMARY
In Genesis 12 v 1-3, God begins to work in the world to fulfil his promise to crush Satan and undo the power of sin and death.

God promises that from Abram, an old man married to a barren woman, will come a family so huge they will be a nation; that they will live in a land God will give them; that Abram and his family will be blessed (ie: be able to enjoy living in God's world under his loving rule, just as humanity was designed to); and that through them, the whole world will one day also be able to know blessing. These promises form a thread running through the rest of the Bible.

Despite the apparent impossibility of these promises, Abram believes God. And he

shows this in his actions—he leaves home, family and community, and travels until God tells him to stop (12 v 7). This is the faith we should copy.

The session moves briefly to Genesis 21 to see God doing the impossible and keeping his promise through the birth of Isaac.

As we move on to John 8, we find Jesus explaining that true children of Abram (or Abraham, as God renamed him) are those who do what he did—trust in God's promises, and obey him in faith.

And Jesus says Abraham looked forward to Jesus time and rejoiced about it. The time of blessing to his family and to the whole world has arrived in the coming of Jesus. He is the One Genesis 12 v 3 looks forward to—the way God keeps his promise.

OPTIONAL EXTRA
Get someone to stand on a chair, facing away from the group. They are going to fall backwards, and the group have to catch them. Give several people a try—some

people simply cannot allow themselves to fall (I can't!). Others can. Discuss what the exercise shows about trust. Ultimately, trust is shown in how you act—here, whether you let yourself fall back or not. Trust is an all-or-nothing thing. You can refer back to this after Q4: Abram showed in his actions his trust in God and his promises. He held nothing back; he gave control to God.

GUIDANCE TO QUESTIONS

1. What, if anything, would persuade you to move permanently away from your… • country? • friends? • family? It's worth underlining the word "permanently"—this isn't a gap year or holiday! The point is that for most people, it would take something very special to make them leave behind all they've ever known.

2. What did God tell Abram to do (v 1)? Leave his country, community and extended family. Go to a land God would show him.

3. What did he promise Abram (v 1-3)?
• **v 1:** He would show him a land to live in.

• **v 2:** Abram would become a great nation ie: his family would end up so big that it would be a nation on its own; his name (reputation/influence) would be great.

• **v 3:** Abram would be blessed (enjoy living in God's world under God's loving rule) and be a blessing (help others to do the same). **Note:** If you did Explore More in Session Two, notice that the builders were grasping at making "a name for ourselves" (11 v 4)—but this is God's gift. The way to a "name" is to obey God. Those who associate with Abram will know God's blessing, and those who oppose him will know God's rejection. Every nation on earth will know blessing through Abram (or his family).

☒

• **How does God make his promises more specific in v 7?** As promised in v 1, he tells Abram the specific area of land he'll give him, once he's got there. It's the land of the Canaanites (v 6)—what is known today as Palestine, or Israel. **Note:** If someone asks whether this means there is still something special about Israel/Palestine, you might like to read Revelation 21 v 1-5, explain that Jerusalem was the capital of Canaan (or Israel as it came to be known), and ask: "Where is the true "land" of God's people?" God's *ultimate* "land" for his people was not a small area east of the Mediterranean—it's the whole world, re-perfected. (See Session Nine.)

4. How does Abram respond (v 4)? How is this a great example of real faith? He goes, because God told him to. Real faith is trusting in God's promises, and obeying him. It is about not putting security in anything else, just simply trusting and following God.

• **Look back at Genesis 11 v 29-30, and compare it with 12 v 2. Why is Abram's response to God's promises particularly impressive?** Abram's wife Sarai could not have children. Yet God was promising Abram a vast family. Abram trusted God to do the humanly impossible. It's harder to trust God when we can't see how he will deliver!

5. APPLY: If we have real faith, as Abram did, how will it show itself in our lives? In obedience. If we trust God (rather than ourselves, or what the world gives us), then we'll obey what he says, no matter what the cost, because we trust that God will do what he has promised, working for our good (see Romans 8 v 28) and bringing us to eternal life (John 10 v 28-30). You can't see faith—but you can see the costly obedience that real faith produces.

6. APPLY: In Abram's time, land, community and family were what people looked to for security in life. What are the things people look to for security today? This will vary depending on your culture. Some ideas: pension plans, family, bank account, house, relationship, insurance, superstition (eg: astrology), job.

- **Where should the Christian look? Why is this hard?** To God, and him alone. This requires giving up control over our lives, and giving up the idea that we can create our own security—that's hard!

- **Does this mean we shouldn't have insurance or pension plans, buy a house, and so on, do you think?** No. We have no command from God to leave these things. But it must mean that we don't look to them as the foundation for our life, or what gives us purpose in life. We must be prepared to leave that kind of western society's security if God calls us to, for instance, move to the developing world as missionaries. It's worth asking: If this thing disappeared overnight, would I be worried or discontented?

7. What do we learn from [Genesis 21 v 1-7] about how God works? He fulfils his promises. He may not do it as quickly as we'd like—this couple had to wait years!

SNAPSHOT

The speech bubble shows this is a promise for the future. The people will live in a good land (grey line, not black), under God's blessing (no line between people and God).

8. It's 1800 years later, and Jesus is talking to members of Abraham's family. But what problem do they all have (v 34-35a)? They are all a "slave to sin"—rejecting God in attitude and action. They couldn't stop sinning even if they wanted. And a slave to sin can't be a part of God's family (v 35a). Though they are physically descended from Abram, spiritually they are not: they are not blessed.

- **What do they need Jesus, God the Son, to do for them (v 36)?** To set them free from slavery to sin, so they are free to belong to God's family again (v 35b).

- **What do they want to do with Jesus (v 40)? What does this show about them (v 39)?** They want to kill him. This shows (v 39) that they're not really Abraham's children at all, because a true child of Abraham would be related to him by action, rather than merely by blood.

9. How are they different to Abraham (v 40—think back to how Abraham reacted to God's words in Genesis 12)? Abraham heard God speaking, knew God was speaking truly, and acted accordingly. These men want to kill the Word who has come from God in the flesh (John 1 v 14).

10. What does Jesus say Abraham did while he was still alive (v 56)? He rejoiced at the prospect of "my day" ie: the time when Jesus would be alive on earth.

- **So what claim is Jesus making for**

himself in **John 8 v 56?** That as Abraham looked forward to the day when God fulfilled his promise to bless the earth, it was actually him, Jesus, that Abraham was looking forward to ie: Jesus is the one who fulfils the promises of Genesis 12.

11. APPLY: Who, today, are the true children of Abraham (v 39, 56)? (Galatians 3 v 29 may help you here.)
• **v 39:** Those who do the things he did ie: trust God's promises and so obey God.
• **v 56:** Those who rejoice at the day God's promises to Abraham were fulfilled—ie: look at Jesus and rejoice.
• **Gal 3 v 29:** Those who "belong to Christ".

12. APPLY: Imagine someone said to you: "Of course I'm a Christian. I've been baptised. I was born into a Christian family. I go to church." What does John 8 have to say to that view? Being a Christian, having God's promised blessing, is not about being part of a particular family, or community, or having gone through a particular rite such as baptism or (in the Old Testament, see Gen 17 v 9-14) circumcision. By nature, we are slaves to sin. We need to

ask the Son, Jesus, to set us free from sin, bring us into God's family, and rejoice that by trusting him we can look forward to life in God's perfect world. That's a Christian!

EXPLORE MORE: Genesis 15 v 1-21 Which two of his promises does God underline here (Gen 15 v 4-5, 7)? Abram will have an heir, and a vast family (v 4-5); he (or his family) will be given the land (v 7). **What further prediction and promise does God make (v 13-15)?** Abram's family will be slaves in another country for four centuries; God will punish that nation, and his family will leave with plunder; Abram will die at peace (before all this happens). **Note:** Exodus 12 v 36 and 40 shows God's promises here being fulfilled (v 36, 40). **What does the writer call this binding agreement God makes with Abram (v 18)?** A covenant. In the Bible, a covenant is a binding agreement made by God to a person/people, in which he makes promises. Sometimes there is a condition (such as in Deuteronomy, where God promises to bless his people if they obey him). Sometimes there isn't—here, for example. God will keep his promises to Abram—no ifs or buts.

Exodus 12; Luke 22

4 DELIVERED FROM JUDGMENT

THE BIG IDEA
Our biggest problem is God's judgment— God rescues us from his judgment by providing his Son to die in our place.

SUMMARY
As God had promised Abraham (Genesis 15 v 13-14), his whole family ended up leaving a famine in Canaan, the land God had

promised to give them, and going to live in Egypt (Genesis 46 v 1-27).

Exodus opens with the Egyptian Pharaoh making Israel slaves. Their newborn sons are killed. One boy who escapes death is Moses. Exodus, Leviticus, Numbers and Deuteronomy are (put simply!) the story of how God worked through his chosen leader, Moses, to rescue his people from slavery, to reveal his character and his standards to them, and to bring them to the verge of the land he'd promised them.

This passage mainly concentrates on how God saves his people from Egypt. Their biggest problem seems to be their slavery, and God promises to solve this (3 v 7-10). But, when Pharaoh refuses to let the people go, God judges everyone in Egypt through the death of their firstborn son. This judgment includes Israel—their greatest problem (and ours) is God's judgment.

But God offers his people a way out. He rescues them from his judgment through a lamb dying in their place, and them daubing the blood on their doorframes (11 v 4 – 12 v 27). Pharaoh releases God's people (12 v 31-32) and God tells them to remember his rescue by eating a Passover meal every year.

We then move to a Passover meal celebrated 1400 years later by Jesus and his friends. Jesus redefines what the meal is about; instead of pointing to the blood of a lamb to rescue Israel from judgment in Egypt, he talks about his blood on the cross, as the ultimate Lamb, rescuing God's people from eternal judgment. God's people are now to share *this* meal together.

Note: The pace picks up in this session. Don't get side-tracked too much—you can always come back in the future!

OPTIONAL EXTRA

After Q6 or at the end of the study, watch the night of the passover in the animation *The Prince of Egypt*: 1:09:20 – 1:13:06.

GUIDANCE FOR QUESTIONS

1. Imagine you surveyed 100 people in your area and asked: What is the biggest problem you face?

Is there a solution to that problem, and what is it? What answers would you get, do you think? Obviously, there are no "right answers" here! You could get things started by giving a couple of suggestions.

2. What does God promise Moses He will do? Rescue them from the Egyptians and bring them to a very good land. He'll do this through Moses (v 10).

- **What does the Israelites' greatest problem appear to be? What solution does God offer?** Their oppression and suffering under their Egyptian slave-drivers. The solution is God acting to free them.

3. What do the Israelites need to do:
- **v 3-5:** Take a perfect year-old lamb (the amount is dictated by the size of family).

- **v 6-7:** Take care of the lamb and then kill it. Put some of the blood on the doorframes of the house.

- **v 8-10:** Eat all of the lamb's meat, with bread without yeast in it.

- **v 11:** Eat the meal having made yourselves completely ready to leave Egypt.

4. Why do they need to do this (v 12-13)? Because the night they do these things, God will kill every firstborn son of every family (human and animal), in judgment on people's rejection of him and worship of other "gods" (v 12). But when God sees a house with blood on the doorframe, he won't kill the firstborn son.

- **What had Pharaoh been doing to the Israelites' children (1 v 15-16)? How does the specific judgment of God here fit the crime?** Pharaoh was killing the firstborn sons of the Israelites—now he and his people lose their firstborn children.

- **So what is really the Israelites' greatest problem? What is the solution?** God's judgment. The solution is the rescue plan of the lamb that God has provided. The crucial point here is that the Israelites need rescuing *from* God—and they are rescued *by* God.

5. What do the Israelites do (v 28)? Exactly what God told them to do.

- **What does God do (v 29)?** Exactly what he said he'd do. All the firstborn not covered by the blood of a lamb die.

- **What does Pharaoh do (v 30-32)?** Exactly what he'd said he wouldn't do! He finally allows God's people to leave.

6. Verse 30 tells us: "There was not a house without someone dead". But in Israelite houses, the firstborn sons had been spared! So how is this verse correct? In any house with a living firstborn son, a lamb had already died. There had to be a death in every house—a son, or a lamb.

- **What does this show about how God rescues people from his judgment?** Through something dying in their place. It's often called a "substitution". The firstborn should die (after all, Israel did not obey God either—they were sinful, including Moses, see 2 v 11-12)—instead, a lamb was substituted and died instead. This is how God rescues people from his judgment—by offering something/someone else to take judgment in the place of the one who deserves it.

7. APPLY: From this study, and the previous ones, what is humanity's greatest problem? God's judgment. We all face his judgment on our sin, our rejection of him—just as Egypt and Israel did. We are not facing the death of our firstborn in one

night—but we will all die (the wages of sin is death, Romans 6 v 23). **Where must we look for the solution?** To God. Our only hope is if he chooses to offer a rescue.

SNAPSHOT
The people are on their way to the land (arrow). They are in relationship with God, but because their sin hasn't been dealt with they don't enjoy full blessing with him (so there's a dotted line in between).

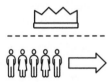

8. What should the people do after their rescue (v 14, 17, 24-25)? Where will they do this, and what should they remember (v 25-27)? Hold a festival which commemorates what God did, in the land God is going to bring them to, to remember that God rescued them from his judgment and from Egyptian slavery. **Note:** This festival has two names: Passover (v 11) and the Festival of Unleavened Bread (v 17).

9. How many times is the word "Passover" mentioned in v 7-13? Four. **Why does the writer, Luke, do this, do you think?** Luke wants us to be thinking about what follows in terms of what the Passover meal was all about—God's rescue from his judgment and Egyptian slavery.

10. During the meal, Jesus takes the bread (v 19), and the wine (v 20) … But what does he say they now represent? His broken body and his poured-out blood.

- **Whose blood does Jesus point his**

followers to? His blood! **Link this back to the events of Exodus. What does this blood achieve?** His death achieved what the lamb's death achieved—the rescue of God's people from God's judgment. As the lamb took the judgment of death that the firstborn deserved, so Jesus takes the judgment of eternal death that we all deserve.

⌄

• **Does Jesus' death automatically rescue all people (think back to the lamb's blood in Egypt)?** No. God offered the lamb as a way the people could be rescued—but they had to obey him by putting the lamb's blood on their doorposts, to show they were trusting in its death. In just the same way, God offers us Jesus as the way to be rescued: we have to obey him by trusting in his blood, by saying that we know that Jesus has delivered us from the death we deserve.

• **Where is the "land" where Jesus is looking forward to eating the Passover meal (v 16, 18)?** "The kingdom of God" when it comes (v 18) in all its fullness. He's looking forward to eating and drinking in a world where God is once more completely recognised as King.

11. What does Jesus tell his followers to do (v 19)? To "do this" (share bread, and also wine) "in remembrance of me" and what he was about to do in dying. **How do his people do this in practice today?** Just as God's people were to look back to Egypt by sharing a meal together, so now God's people should look back to the cross by sharing a meal together. We do this every time we share bread and wine in a way which consciously remembers Jesus' broken

body and poured-out blood—Communion / the Lord's Supper / Eucharist.

Note: There are a wide variety of approaches to this meal. It has different names; is celebrated in different ways; and is eaten with different frequencies. The crucial thing is that the focus is on remembering what Jesus has done in dying on the cross, rescuing us from God's judgment.

12. APPLY: Use the events of the Passover in Egypt to explain to someone else in the group what Jesus achieved on the cross. Key points:
• People need rescuing from God's judgment. In Egypt, firstborn sons faced death; ultimately everyone faces death, separation from God and his blessing.
• God provides a rescue by offering a substitute—someone who doesn't deserve to die, dying in the place of one who does.
• The ultimate substitute is Jesus, his perfect Son, who died in our place, just as the lambs died in place of the firstborn sons.
• As the Israelites trusted in the lamb's blood to deliver their firstborn from death, so we need to trust in Jesus' blood to deliver us.
• They were to remember how God had rescued them in Egypt by sharing a meal. We are to do the same to remember how God delivered us from death at the cross.

13. APPLY: What should we be thinking about, and how should we be feeling, when we share Communion? *Thinking about:* the cross, where Jesus rescued us (Luke 22 v 19-20); our future, when we will eat with Jesus in his kingdom (v 16, 18). *Feeling:* all sorts of things! But not *nothing*. Communion should engage our emotions as well as our thoughts. Deep sorrow over our sin, which took Jesus to the cross; huge gratitude that he went there; great excitement at sharing his kingdom; real determination to live as part of his people. These are all feelings we may experience as we take Communion. At different times in our lives and circumstances, it may be that one of these feelings is particularly real to us.

EXPLORE MORE: Exodus 20 v 1-17
What is it [that God has already done] (Exodus 20 v 2)? Brought (or rescued) them from slavery in Egypt.
What comes first—being rescued by God, or obeying him? Being rescued.
Why is this crucial to remember? If we have been saved by God (through the blood of the lamb then, and Jesus now), then we live his way *in response* to that, and because we want to know the blessing of living God's way in God's place. But we don't live God's way *so that* we can be saved.
Read through the Commandments. Which does your society generally agree with, and which does it reject? Most western societies agree with 5–10, though they might make exceptions to six, seven (eg: abortion) and nine. 1–4, which focus on how to relate to God, are pretty unpopular!

5 Judges 2; 2 Samuel 7; Mark 8 – 9
EVER-REIGNING KING

THE BIG IDEA
We need a King to lead us to live God's way and enjoy his blessing—and who will never die. We need King Jesus.

SUMMARY
This session looks first at Judges. Moses has died, the people have entered the God-promised land under Joshua, and are starting to enjoy blessing. But God's people throw it all away, and in Judges 2 we are introduced to an interminable cycle:

• They worship other "gods" (v 10-13).
• God judges them—their enemies are able to invade and occupy the land (v 14-15).
• They cry out to God (v 15, see also 3 v 9).
• God rescues them by raising up a judge, to defeat their enemies and lead them in obeying God (2 v 16-18).
• The judge dies, and the people return to worshipping other gods again (v 19).

As things get worse, four times we're told: "In those days Israel had no king" (17 v 6, 18 v 1, 19 v 1, 21 v 25). The people need a leader powerful enough to rescue and lead them under God's rule; they need a leader who won't die, and leave them to turn back to other gods and face judgment again.

After the reign of disobedient King Saul, God chooses a good king for his people — David. David is the "anointed one", the "messiah" (NIV2011) or "christ" (NIV84).

David is a great king—but in 2 Samuel 7 v 4-16, God promises there will one day be a far greater king from David's family. He will rule perfectly, for ever—and he will uniquely be called God's son. His kingdom will be one of rest and blessing for God's people—and since he will rule for ever, it will never end.

This Messiah—*the* Messiah—did not come until a thousand years later. But one of the friends of Jesus of Nazareth (a descendant of David) realised that Jesus was this Messiah (Mark 8 v 29); and his opinion was immediately confirmed by God himself, who calls Jesus his Son (9 v 7).

So this study focuses on Jesus as ruler, rather than as rescuer. He is the all-powerful, divine, awesome Messiah, the fulfilment of God's promises to David. We would do well to worship and obey such a Man.

GUIDANCE TO QUESTIONS

1. Have you ever found yourself making the same mistake repeatedly, even though you resolve each time not to do it again? What made it so hard to stop? What would have helped you? It doesn't matter if answers are flippant ("I keep locking my keys in the car—I need a new brain!") or serious ("I kept getting angry with my children—I needed counselling").

2. What happened after Joshua died?
- **v 10-13:** God's people, Israel, turned away from God, worshipping the "gods" of nearby nations—angering the true God.
- **v 14-15:** God "gave them into the hands" of their enemies; they were defeated.
- **v 16:** God raised up judges (or leaders) to save Israel from their enemies.

3. What was the advantage of having a God-given judge (v 18)? The judge was the way God had compassion on his sinful, suffering people; during the judge's life, the people were safe from their enemies.
- **What was the problem (v 19-21)?** "The judge died". And then "the people returned" to sinning again (v 19), so God responded in judgment (v 20-21).

4. Read Judges 17 v 6, 18 v 1, 19 v 1, 21 v 25. What does the writer of Judges suggest is the basic cause, and the solution to, Israel's troubles? To save time, you could give your group a verse each to look up. Two verses say: "Everyone did as they saw fit"—the cause of all the problems.

All four say: "Israel had no king". The solution is to have a king, powerful enough to lead the people effectively in obeying God, to rule them as God wanted, so that everyone did not simply do as they wanted or thought best (17 v 6, 21 v 25).

5. APPLY: What does Judges 2 (and the whole book) tell us about what God's people are like? God's people are sinful, despite all God's blessings. They quickly turn from worshipping God to worshipping what the world around them does. They need strong leadership and good rule if they are to follow God and experience his blessings.

- **Do we see this today? How?** Make sure your group are talking about the church (ie: those who call themselves God's people), rather than the world (those who don't), and then let the group discuss this as they wish. The conclusion will probably be "yes"—we are still sinful! We still turn away from God, and the church is still attracted to believing and acting like the society around it. God's people today still suffer when leadership is weak in teaching and insisting on what is truly right.

6. APPLY: What does it tell us about the benefits and limitations of human leaders? *Benefits:* Human leaders in the church and state can be used by God. We should not be instinctively mistrustful of authority. God uses people to establish peace and prosperity.
Limitations: Human leaders, even God-given ones like the judges, cannot deal with the problem of our sin, our natural inclination to turn away from God. The best, most faithful leader of a nation or a church will not produce perfect people. And they will die, and cease to rule. No human leader can be the answer to our problems.

7. What will happen to David himself (2 Samuel 7 v 12a)? He will die: the "days" of his rule will be "over". **Why does this matter? (Hint: Think back to the problem with the judges.)** Because we need a ruler who won't be replaced—won't die—whose perfect, unending rule will mean God's people can live under God's rule, enjoying his blessing. David is great, but (like the judges) he is not the ultimate solution.

8. But what does God promise about one of his descendants?

• **v 12:** God will establish his rule/kingdom.

• **v 13, 16:** His throne will be "established for ever". This could mean David's line will always rule, but more likely it's referring to a king who will himself rule for all time. **Note:** God says David's descendant will "build a house for my Name" (v 13), ie: a temple where God is particularly present. This was in part fulfilled by Solomon, David's son, who built the Jerusalem temple. But this was never the final fulfilment, as proved by its destruction 400 years later. The ultimate "house for my Name", where God fully dwells on earth, is Jesus, who talked about himself as the temple (see John 2 v 19-22). For more on the partial, yet incomplete, fulfilment of God's promises to David in the reign of Solomon, see *Explore More*.

⌄

• **Read Isaiah 9 v 6-7. 400 years later, God is giving details about what this ruling descendant of David will do and be like. What do we discover?**
  • He will be God himself (v 6).
  • There will be no end to the rule and peace he brings (v 7).
  • He will rule David's kingdom, for ever (v 7). Verse 7 makes clear that when God promises a king for ever, he means one particular ruling "Messiah".

• **v 14-15:** This successor will have a unique father-son relationship with God. And, strangely, while he will be punished for doing wrong, God's love will never be removed from him.
If your group ask about this—and there is time—ask how this prophecy is fulfilled in Jesus. The answer is at the cross, where Jesus became sinful, by taking our sin on himself, and was punished for that wrongdoing (see 2 Corinthians 5 v 21).

• **What else does God promise David (v 10-11)?** He will give his people, David's subjects, an undisturbed home (v 10); rest from their enemies (v 11).

SNAPSHOT

The people are now in the good, though not perfect (so grey, not black) land that God has given them. And he has given them a king to lead them in obedience to him.

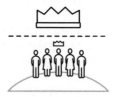

9. What does Peter recognise about Jesus? "You are the Messiah" or "Christ" (Mark 8 v 29); David's descendant promised in 2 Samuel 7.

⌄

• **Read Matthew 1 v 1-17 (possibly best done silently—the names are tricky!). How does this show that Peter might be right in identifying Jesus as David's descendant who is the Messiah?** Jesus was in David's family tree, and in Abraham's. He could be the fulfilment of the promises of both Genesis

12 v 1-3, made to Abraham about one of his descendants, and of 2 Samuel 7, made about someone descended from David.

10. How does 9 v 2-8 show that Peter is right? Jesus is seen, briefly, in all his power and heavenly royal glory (v 2-3). A cloud, signifying God's presence, appears and the Father confirms that this is his Son (v 7), who should be listened to ie: heard and obeyed. In a way, this is God saying to Peter and anyone else who identifies Jesus as the Messiah: "Yes, you are right."

• **Given what God promised David, why is this seriously exciting?!** Jesus is the one Israel had waited for, for 1000 years. He is the one who will rule, perfectly, for ever, as God's Son and Messiah, rescuing and ruling his people under God. He is the central figure of history.

11. Remember, the central flaw with both the judges and with David is that, though they may lead God's people to obey God for a while, eventually they die. Why is what Jesus predicts in v 9 so crucial? Jesus (referring to himself here as the "Son of Man") would rise from the dead. Death would not be the end of his rule. So not only can he rule God's people perfectly, he can also rule them eternally.

12. APPLY: Why is it good to obey Jesus? Why is it right to do so? Why do we find it hard to?
• It's good because his rule is the one which brings blessing, and does so eternally. We will not find that in any other human leader, authority or opinion-former.
• It's right because he is the all-powerful King of heaven and earth. We should be in awe of him. His status both deserves and demands our obedience.

• It's hard because we are sinful! Like the people in Judges, we naturally reject God and live our own way. We need consciously to obey Jesus even when we don't feel like it or it is not what we would naturally have done.

OPTIONAL EXTRA
To reinforce the point that Jesus is unique because he alone was not defeated, and his influence not ended, by death, watch *Jesus is alive* by the US rapper Shai Linne. At the time of press, you can find it at: http://www.youtube.com/watch?v=BauJLUTxxZo

EXPLORE MORE: 1 Kings 4, 11 [From 1 Kings 4 v 20-34] Pick out the verses which suggest Solomon might be the fulfilment of God's promises.
• **v 20:** Abraham's descendants are a numerous people.
• **v 20:** They are happy (a sign of blessing)
• **v 21:** Solomon's rule is secure, and other nations are subject to him—Israel is a "great nation" (Genesis 12 v 2).
• **v 25:** God's people are enjoying the blessing of peace and safety.
• **v 29-31:** Solomon is wiser than any other human.
• **v 31, 34:** Solomon's wisdom was a blessing to other nations.

What happened to Solomon (11 v 1-8)? He married foreign women (v 1), who God had warned his people not to marry because they worshipped other gods and would lead Israel to do the same (v 2). This is exactly what Solomon ended up doing (v 4-8).

How did God react (v 9-13)? "The LORD became angry" (v 9). His judgment was that the kingdom would be divided (v 11-13).

6 Amos 8 – 9; Luke 23
FUTURE BEYOND JUDGMENT

THE BIG IDEA

God is a God who judges sin, and who promises his people a wonderful future. At the cross, God's Son took God's judgment for us, so that we can look forward to a wonderful life in his perfect kingdom.

SUMMARY

Put together, the prophets cover the time from the first kings to the end of the Old Testament, four centuries before Jesus was born—a huge period of history! In that time, the kingdom split into two (Israel in the north; Judah in the south). Israel (in 722BC) and Judah (in 596BC) were invaded, destroyed and the people exiled; but a small number of Judeans returned to rebuild Jerusalem and its temple. Throughout, God spoke to his people through his prophets. They did not only foretell the future; they also explained the present.

Each prophet warns God's people to stop rejecting him, explains what it is that is angering God, and warns them what God will do in response—that *judgment is coming*. But each prophet also promises that God will somehow restore his people, and fulfil God's promises in a way which surpasses even the high point of David and Solomon—that *salvation will follow*.

The exile was a catastrophic judgment on the people. Yet it was not final—God brought a remnant of his people back to the land. But this future beyond judgment was not the life God had promised; and the prophets who lived after this return were still exposing the ongoing sin of God's people. The Old Testament ends with warnings that judgment is still coming; and with God's

people still looking to the future salvation and final fulfilment of his promises.

This study focuses on one particular prophet, Amos. And then it moves through 400 years of silence to reach the time of Jesus the Messiah. In his death, he experienced the full, final judgment of complete exile from God's presence. In taking that judgment for others, he gave God's people the future the prophets had promised: the future of paradise, an eternal life in God's presence.

1. What do you most look forward to in life? Funny and serious answers welcome, but make sure there are a few of the latter! Answers will range from more immediate events, such as a holiday or the weekend, to those further off—for some, it may be retirement, for others having a family.

- **How does that affect your feelings and actions in the present?** Allow people to spend time working this out. The point is that if we really do look forward to something, it makes us feel different (hopeful, excited, satisfied in advance), and we even act differently (eg: if we're on holiday next week, it will spur us to work hard now, keeping going on our tasks till we get there).

2. How does Israel treat obeying God's laws, such as resting on the Sabbath (v 5)? They pay lip service to them. But their hearts are on other things, namely making money. They do the bare minimum of obedience, and it makes no difference beyond the Sabbath and festival days.

- **How do those with more wealth treat those with less (v 4, 6)?** They happily tread on them to get themselves to the top (v 4). They see them as items to be bought and sold (v 6).

3. Sum up what God tells Israel he'll do:

- **v 10:** He will turn celebrations into times for mourning. "An only son" would be the great hope of the family—so this pictures a time when there is absolutely no hope.

- **v 11-12:** He will withdraw knowledge and understanding of his word. People will realise they need to hear from God—but it will be too late. Part of God's judgment on a nation that does not want his word is that they won't have his word!

- **v 14:** Death will come to those who worship other gods.

4. What will be the sign that God's judgment has arrived (v 9)?
The sun won't shine in the middle of the day—it will go dark.

5. APPLY: How might the attitudes shown in 8 v 4-6 look in your church and your life today?
The religion of "Sunday worship" is still alive and well, where we do and say the right things in church one day a week, and forget about God from Monday to Saturday. Often we cut corners, undermining what is right in order to do what will increase profits, getting away with what we can in order to make a living. And how often do we ignore those less fortunate than ourselves, in our own country and others, because we are too busy getting even more for ourselves?

- **What would the opposite (true godliness) look like?** You might like to get your group to rewrite verses 4-6 but as the opposite: something like:
"Hear this, you who help the needy and make sure the poor of the land are not

forgotten about, saying: 'Let us focus on celebrating the New Moon festival and trust in God for providing what we need, and keep the Sabbath without worrying about missing out on work hours— making sure we are scrupulously honest even at cost to ourselves, and that we care more about doing what is right than doing what is profitable, giving our silver to the poor and valuing them as people, not products.'"
Talk about specific ways your group do this, struggle with this, and need to change to obey God in this.

If you want to include the Explore More section (see end of Study Guide), here would be a good place to do it.

6. What will God do to David's fallen kingdom "in that day" (v 11)?
Restore it, repair it, make it as it was before his judgment came.

- **What will be different about the extent of the kingdom (v 12)?** It won't be limited to the borders of Israel. Edom was a nation to the north of Old Testament Israel (and one of its greatest enemies). God's people will "possess" it— that is, live there too—and they will live throughout the world, in every nation.

- **What will life be like for God's people (v 13-15)?** Verses 13-14 give a picture of plenty and abundance, of the world working for humans rather than against them (a reversal of the curse of Genesis 3 v 17-19, see Session Two). V 15 introduces the idea of eternity, that there will be no more struggle or exile. Clearly, by this stage the issue of the people's constant sin will have been completely dealt with, though we are given no idea how. Notice it's God who will do these things: it's

God who brings his people there, and keeps them there. Heaven comes to earth through God's actions, not humanity's.

SNAPSHOT

There will be fewer people without a land, king or relationship with God—but one day, there will be many people in a wonderful world under the perfect rule of God's King.

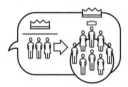

7. Why is the mocking sign above Jesus' head both ironic and tragic? Because he *was* King of the Jews! He was the perfect Jew, who always lived God's way; and the chosen Jew, God's Messiah. Yet tragically, God's people decided to kill the Messiah.

8. How does Amos' prophecy help us understand what's happening in v 44-45a? The sixth hour is (in our timings) midday. This is exactly what Amos 8 v 9 foretold. It is a sign that God's judgment has come. A time of hopelessness, withdrawal of his presence (or word) and death has arrived. And the shock is that it is God's Messiah, Jesus, dying under this judgment.

⌄

• Israel is crucifying God's Messiah, Jesus. Who would we expect God's judgment to fall upon at this point? His executors! If ever an act deserved divine judgment, it is the killing of the Father's Son.

9. Look at verse 45. What does this show Jesus' death has achieved?

Everything that was blocking relationship between God and people—our sin—has been dealt with.

10. What does the second criminal dying next to Jesus recognise about him, and ask him to do? That Jesus (unlike him) is innocent, and not deserving of death (neither Roman crucifixion, nor the judgment of God). And he asks Jesus to remember him when he comes into his kingdom. It's worth teasing out what else the thief is recognising about Jesus here—that he is a King, and that his kingdom lies beyond death. You may need to add that for God, or his King, to "remember" is not only to remember, but also to act. So the criminal is not just saying: "Please remember me" but "Please act to bring me into your kingdom".

• **What does Jesus promise him about his future?** That he will do what the criminal has asked: bring him into his kingdom, paradise, with him.

• **How can someone experience the ultimate fulfilment of God's promises in the prophets, like Amos 9 v 11-15?** By recognising that Jesus is the King of God's kingdom, the ultimate descendant of David, and by asking him for a place in that kingdom. All that God has promised throughout the OT is fulfilled in the kingdom-beyond-death of Jesus Christ, so all God has promised can be experienced and enjoyed by anyone who trusts Jesus to take them there to be with him.
You might point out the promises of Amos 9 are very "earthy"—life here, on this earth. And that is where all Jesus' subjects are destined for, though they wait with him in "paradise" beyond death for the time when God remakes this world. Bear in mind this is the subject of Session Nine!

11. APPLY: Imagine that someone had (for some reason!) read Amos 8 – 9, and wanted to know what it all means for us today. How would you explain to them what Amos tells us about... A chance to check each others' understanding, and talk about how the OT points to Jesus.

- **what the Lord Jesus' death saves people *from*?** It saves people who trust in him from the horrific judgment of God on those who rebel against him, including rebelling by doing the right thing on a Sunday (=Sabbath) and at Christmas and Easter (=New Moon) but who don't live God's way the rest of the time (that is, to a greater or lesser extent, all of us!) We face hopelessness, exile from God's presence, and death—and Jesus takes all of that from his people as he dies.

- **what the Lord Jesus' death saves people *for*?** It opens up a wonderful future for anyone who knows and trusts Jesus, because in taking our death, Jesus gives us a place in his kingdom with him. A future which will never end, a future of great plenty, a future which is totally secure, a future in this world experiencing better than anything we've known so far.

12. APPLY: What should we be looking forward to most? Life in Jesus' kingdom, enjoying being with him and experiencing life in God's place, as his people, blessed by him! It's where all Jesus' people are headed. **If we do, how will it affect our feelings and actions now?** In many ways, including: **Feelings:** *Joy* even when life is tough, because we know what lies ahead for us. *Peace* even when life doesn't go as we hoped, because we know that one day life will be everything we could ever hope for. *Not worrying*, because we know Jesus has secured our future. *Gratitude* each day to

Jesus for what he's given us, and a desire to serve him. *Determination* to keep living with Jesus as our King and Saviour.
Actions: *Telling others* how they can avoid judgment and enjoy the future we're headed for. *Living obediently* as part of King Jesus' kingdom now. *Giving up/away* things people look to now in order to make them secure eg: promotion, possessions, popularity, because we know Jesus has already bought an amazing future with his blood.

EXPLORE MORE: 2 Kings 17 v 1-13, 18-20 What happened (2 Kings 17 v 3-6)? The King of Assyria (a local superpower) invaded Israel, besieged the capital, Samaria, took it and deported the people to places far away. **That's the human, political perspective—what was going on under the surface (v 18-20)?** God's judgment had come, as the prophets had warned. Israel was leaving "his presence", the land he'd given them to live in and enjoy his rule and blessing. **Why (v 7-9a)?** Because "the Israelites had sinned" (v 7), by: worshipping other gods; copying nations who rejected God; doing things that "were not right" (v 9) ie: went against how God had told them to live. **How is what is happening here the opposite of God's promises to Abraham of people, land and blessing?** The people are plundered (v 20); taken far from the land (v 6); and removed from God's presence, where he blesses his people (v 20).

- **to David, of a king who would rule under God, and for ever?** Hoshea and his fathers didn't rule under God (v 2); this king was defeated and ceased to rule (v 6). **How does this section underline how awful it is to face God's judgment?** It is to experience the opposite of how we were created to live. It is to be far from home, people, safety, security, prosperity. It is to be left without hope (v 23).

7 Luke 9, 24
GOD IN HIS WORLD

THE BIG IDEA

Jesus is God's promised Messiah, the One who fulfilled all God's promises—and his resurrection proves that he is.

SUMMARY

In this session, we (at last!) reach the New Testament Gospels. Having focused on various aspects of Jesus' ministry in each previous session, including seeing how the cross is where God keeps his promise to deliver us from judgment and give us a future beyond judgment (Sessions Four and Six), here we focus on the resurrection.

The resurrection of Jesus, foretold by him several times (Luke 9 v 21-22, 44-45; 18 v 31-34) is the proof that his words are true. The resurrection shows that what Jesus says, happens—as the angels at his tomb point out to the women: "Remember how he told you" (24 v 6). In a sense, that's the foundation of the Christian life. We remember and live by what Jesus told us.

Which means:

- we know that God has fulfilled his Old Testament promises to his people through Jesus, the Creator, the snake-crusher, the blessing-bringer, the substitutionary lamb, the ever-reigning King, the One who gives us life beyond judgment.

- we trust Jesus' promises—this session picks up on two, that forgiveness is now available to anyone (24 v 47), and that the Holy Spirit ("power from on high") is given to his people (v 49—we look at the Spirit in more detail in the next session).

- we give our lives to Jesus, giving up what is easiest or most comfortable or safest

or even what seems sensible in order to follow him and live under his rule. We'll only really do this if we really know who Jesus is—and the resurrection is where we find the confidence to really know.

OPTIONAL EXTRA

Write down a list of promises on a sheet to give to everyone. Make some serious, and some flippant, and relying on a range of different abilities to fulfil. Eg: I will bake you a fantastic cake tomorrow… I will strip down, clean and reassemble your car engine… I will do your job for a week… I will look after your elderly relatives / young children while you're away on a work trip / holiday… I will buy you a Mars Bar on 13th April next year. Have a few more promises than you have members in your group. Get people to write down who in the group they'd most trust to fulfil each of the promises. Then go through, asking them why they've chosen each person. Finish by asking what we trust Jesus to do, and not do (we don't trust him to bake us a cake tomorrow!)—and why we trust him to do certain things, and not others.

GUIDANCE TO QUESTIONS

1. In this session, we (finally!) reach the New Testament. What promises has God made through the Old Testament?
This is an opportunity to recap and revise(!) the promises we've seen God making in previous sessions.
One: To make a very good world, with people living under God's loving rule.
Two: To send someone to defeat the devil and death.

Three: To bring blessing to people from all over the world.

Four: To deliver God's people from his judgment by providing someone/something to die in our place.

Five: To give his people an eternal King, to lead his people in obeying him.

Six: To bring his people to a wonderful life beyond his judgment.

2. What are the options as to who Jesus is (v 19-20)?

• John the Baptist (Jesus' cousin, a prophet, who announced Jesus' arrival)
• Elijah (a hugely important OT prophet)
• another prophet

All of these mean: a holy man, close to God.

• the Messiah, God's chosen, all-powerful, eternal, promised King

• **What options do people come up with today?**

3. Have a look at these passages and think about... • how they suggest that Peter's verdict is the correct one.
• **how they show Jesus fulfilling a promise of God.**

It would probably be best to split into pairs and give each pair one or two of these sections to look at and "report back" on:

• **Luke 4 v 33-37:** Jesus has power over evil spirits (the head of which is the devil). The evil spirit knows Jesus is "the Holy One of God"—not just a holy man, but God himself. Here is the promised devil-crusher.

• **5 v 12-16:** Jesus can heal effortlessly. He doesn't need to pray or do it in the name of God, like miracle-working prophets or (in Acts) apostles—he does it himself. In the OT, leprosy was a disease which excluded people from the people of God (Leviticus 13 v 42-46); here Jesus,

is reversing this, bringing the leper the blessing of being part of God's people.

• **5 v 17-26:** Jesus can forgive sins, and proves he has this authority by performing a visible healing. The question in v 21 is a good one—only God can forgive sins, so that people don't face his judgment. Jesus is delivering this man from judgment.

• **7 v 1-10:** Jesus can heal someone he's not physically with! And he does it for a Roman, a hated occupier. Jesus brings blessing to people from all nations.
Note: When Jesus lived on earth, the land where God's ancient people lived was all called Israel—there was no distinction made between "Israel" and "Judah", as there was in Amos' time (previous session).

• **7 v 11-17:** Jesus can raise someone from the dead. Unlike the rare times God works through someone else to raise someone (eg: 1 Kings 17 v 17-24), Jesus raises this man in his own power. He is a "great prophet"—*and* "God ... come to help his people" (v 16). He can defeat death.

• **8 v 22-25:** Jesus has power over creation. His word controls weather. He is bigger than any category his followers have: "Who is this?" they ask (v 25). He brings this chaotic, imperfect world into calm and peace and perfection.

4. What four things does Jesus promise will happen to him (v 22)? Suffering; rejection by the leaders of God's people Israel; be killed; rise again three days later.
Note: In first-century Israel, part days counted as whole days. So Jesus rose three days after dying—Friday, Saturday, Sunday.

• **Imagine you were a friend of Jesus the Messiah, listening to him. You know what God has promised he will do through his ever-lasting King. How would you feel about what Jesus says here?** There's no "right answer"—but we can safely guess the disciples must have been shocked. God's King had come to die as a failure! And they may well have been disappointed—this isn't what you imagine an all-powerful, eternal King doing! See Mark 8 v 32 for Peter's reaction!

5. Read Luke 9 v 23-26. How is the life His followers will experience similar to His own?

• They will deny themselves (v 23)—what seems easiest/best for them—as Jesus did.

• They will take up a metaphorical cross (v 23)—being rejected by the world, worthy of death—just as Jesus really did.

• They will "lose" their life (v 24), being willing to give up anything in life, and even life itself, to follow Jesus—just as Jesus lost his life for his people.

• They will know that by losing their life for Jesus, they will save their life eternally (v 24)—just as Jesus lost his life, knowing there was a future beyond death (v 22).

• In a world which rejects Jesus and his words, they will not be ashamed of Jesus or what he says (v 26).

• **What promise does Jesus make (v 24)?** Whoever loses their life for him, letting him be in charge of it, will save it—will have eternal life.

6. APPLY: What would the world around you make of verse 24? Why? The world is focused on keeping hold of life, and grasping at what we can get in this life. We're encouraged to concentrate on getting what we can—experiences, possessions, relationships. It is a crazy idea to entrust our life to someone else, to be willing to give up everything, to go through anything, to lose even life itself, for that person—particularly when that person lived 2,000 years ago.

• **When do we find it hardest to live by verse 24? Why?** Keep your group

focused on their own lives and on specific circumstances. The idea is not to talk about how hard it would be if we lived in a different place, or at a different time (though the Christian life is far harder in non-western, non-21st-century contexts), but to think about when it's hard to give up what's easiest or most comfortable or safest for *us*—in *our* social lives, decision-making, relationships, work setting, etc.

7. Jesus has been buried, but his tomb is empty. Why, according to the angels (v 5-6)? He isn't dead, he's living (v 5); he is risen!

8. Pick out the things that happen in these two passages which give us confidence that Jesus had really risen from the dead.

• **v 3:** His body was not in the tomb (which demands an explanation).

• **v 5-6:** The angels said he'd risen.

• **v 6-8:** He's predicted it (though you can leave this point to Q9).

• **v 11:** The disciples didn't believe it at first; they were in no mindset to steal the body.

• **v 12:** The grave clothes were left behind (grave robbers would have taken them).

• **v 39:** The risen Jesus had flesh and bones, and could be touched (not a hallucination).

• **v 42-43:** The risen Jesus ate (his was a real, human body).

9. Why should the women at the tomb have known Jesus would rise (v 6-7)? Because he'd told them he would. What Jesus promises, happens.

• **Why should the men in the room have known he would rise (v 44, 46)?** Because the "Law of Moses, the Prophets and the Psalms" (the Old Testament) are all about him; and they predicted his suffering and his resurrection.

⊡

• How do these passages predict Jesus' suffering and resurrection: Isaiah 53; Psalm 22.

10. What does Jesus promise his followers is now available (v 47, 49)?
• **v 47:** Forgiveness of sins "in his name". Because of who Jesus is and what he's done (his "name"), people who repent —turn back to God's loving rule—can be forgiven their sins. And this is for "all nations": this blessing of life with God is open to people all over the world.
• **v 49:** "Power from on high" is a reference to the Holy Spirit (see Acts 2 v 1-4). God will now live with and in his people (you don't need to go into too much detail here, as this is a big part of Session Eight).

11. APPLY: What does the resurrection prove about...
• **Jesus' identity?** He is who he said he was, who Peter recognized him as—the Messiah, God come to his world.
• **Jesus' words?** What he says is true. We can trust absolutely everything he said about every part of life, death and eternity.
• **Jesus' promises?** What he promises, he will do. We can trust that, if we've repented and come under his loving rule, we are forgiven. We can trust that his Holy Spirit is in us. And we can trust his promises about the future—that we will be with him when we die (23 v 42-43); that he will return one day in power (17 v 24) and free his people (21 v 28).

12. APPLY: How should Jesus' resurrection from the dead change the way we look at our lives:
• **now?** We should be willing to give up

anything, including our life, for him.
• **in the future?** We can be absolutely certain he will save us, and that we will enjoy all that God has promised—perfect life in his perfect world, because Jesus has taken our judgment and risen to rule us.

SNAPSHOT
Jesus is the Messiah, who's taken away the barrier of sin between his people and God.

EXPLORE MORE: Luke 20 v 9-19
What has God asked for; and how has Israel responded (Luke 20 v 9-12)? For his rights—recognition that he is in charge of his world. Israel has refused to live under his rule, and refused to listen to each prophet.
What awful decision does Israel then make (v 13-15)? To kill the Son, so they can get on with life in the world without God.
What will God do next (v 16)? The tenants will be punished, with no place in the world. God will give it to others to enjoy.
Jesus' crucifixion is what's being talked about in verse 15. What should we expect to see happening next (v 16)? Judgment for his ancient people, who have decisively rejected him. Others coming into relationship with him, inheriting his promised, perfect, eternal world.
How is this story both a warning and an exciting promise? Warning: Not to refuse to recognise and obey God's Son, Jesus, as we live in his Father's world.
Promise: Through knowing Jesus as God's Son, we can enjoy God's perfect vineyard.

8 Acts 1 – 2
HEAR THE MESSAGE

THE BIG IDEA

God has given his Son's followers his Spirit, to enable them to take the message about Jesus all over his world and to live as part of his church.

SUMMARY

We've reached our own time! Living between Jesus' ascension and return (Acts 1 v 11), God's people are part of his mission to the world—to take the gospel about his Son's life, death and resurrection from Jerusalem to the "ends of the earth" (v 8).

To do this, Jesus sends his Spirit to us to give us the power, courage and words to tell people about him. In Acts 2, we see the Spirit come to the first Christians—and we immediately see him empower Jesus' followers to share the gospel message.

This study also looks at the church, the body of believers into which the Spirit calls the people he saves. Acts 2 v 42-47 shows what true church community is, and the way God uses the community's witness to save people.

The aim of this session is to excite Christians today about being part of God's plan, the way he brings to all areas of his world the wonderful message that he has fulfilled his promises in his Son; and to challenge us to share his priorities—to make witnessing about his Son, and being devoted to our church, what we spend our lives doing.

The *Explore More* section is particularly helpful this session, as it points us to the Spirit's work *in* us in Galatians 5 v 15-25, a helpful addition to the main focus of the study, which is the Spirit's work *through* us.

OPTIONAL EXTRA

Share resources which help share the gospel. Eg: Christianity Explored's *Jesus: Who Why What?* booklets, or some *Two ways to live* gospel outlines. Go to www.thegoodbook. co.uk/outreach/christianityexplored/books-and-tracts/jesus, or www.thegoodbook. co.uk/outreach/outreach-courses/two-ways-to-live. Alternatively, point your group to a biblical, clear and friendly evangelistic website like www.christianityexplored.org

GUIDANCE TO QUESTIONS

1. Being in heaven is better than being in this present world. All Christ's followers will have life in heaven. So why do you think God doesn't take Christians to heaven now?! This is to help us think about a strange, but very good question: why doesn't God simply take to heaven anyone who comes to faith in him? Why the gap between conversion and glory? At this stage, there's no "right" answer!

2. Circle on the map the areas Jesus mentions in verse 8. Circle Jerusalem; Judea, the surrounding area; Samaria, to the north; the ends of the earth (map edges!).

3. Imagine you are one of the handful of followers Jesus has at this point. How would you feel about the prospect of obeying the second half of verse 8, do you think?! There are many possible answers to this. But here are a few Christians, who have probably never left Israel; who have seen their Master horribly tortured and executed while they deserted and denied him; who are a tiny minority in

Jewish-dominated Jerusalem; who are now being told they are to start the process of taking the message about Jesus to the whole world. Terror, inadequacy, hopelessness at the size of the task, wondering how to start… would be how I'd feel!

- **Why would the first half of verse 8 be a great comfort to you?** They will not have to do this impossible-sounding mission alone. God himself, the Holy Spirit, will come to them and give them power.

4. What do the "men dressed in white" say is the next major event in God's plan, following the "ascension"? Jesus will return from God's presence in the same way he entered it. The next event on God's timeline is the return of the Lord Jesus.

⌄

- **What era of God's plan do we live in today?** The same as those people there that day! We live between Jesus Christ's ascension and return.

Note: If you have time, read Acts 2 v 1-41 at this point (not just three short chunks of Acts 2), noticing how Peter tells the crowd that Jesus is the one who fulfils the promises of the Old Testament (v 16-21, 25-31, v 34-36).

5. … What do these verses [v 1-4] tell us about who he is, and what he does? People may not pick out all of these! Key point: The Spirit is God, living in Christians.

- A wind-like sound comes from heaven (v 1)—the Spirit comes from God.
- The Spirit fills the house (v 2)—while he does (as we're about to see) dwell in Christians, he is not limited to them. he is at work throughout his world.
- They see tongues of fire (v 3). In the Old

Testament, fire is a sign of God's presence (eg: Exodus 19 v 18). The Spirit *is* God.

- The fire rested on each Christian (v 3). The Spirit dwells in *all* Christians (there were 120 of them at this point, 1 v 15)—not only "special" believers. Notice the fire rests on the Christians, and yet they survive. In the Old Testament, fire was a physical sign that imperfect humans could not survive in God's holy presence (Exodus 19 v 20-21). Now, they can. What has changed matters is the cross, where God's punishment on sin fell on Christ so people could live with God (shown by the temple curtain tearing, Luke 23 v 44-46).
- All of them were filled with the Spirit (v 4). *Every* Christian is full of the Spirit.
- The Spirit enables the believers to speak in tongues ie: foreign languages (v 4; v 7-8 makes clear these were human languages).

⌄

- **What is the mission Jesus gave these Christians (1 v 8)?** These Christians are to take the message about Jesus to people who don't speak Aramaic, their native tongue. **How is the Spirit in 2 v 4 equipping them to begin this mission?** He is giving them the ability to do this. **Note:** V 4 is not what we should expect to happen whenever someone becomes a Christian. The Spirit equips and encourages us all to witness about Jesus— but not necessarily in the same ways.

6. How does the Spirit-filled Peter start doing what Jesus had asked in 1 v 8? He begins to tell people about Jesus. In v 22-24, he recounts the crucial details of the gospel: that Jesus was no mere man (v 22); he was killed by people, but as part of God's plan (v 23); he was raised from the dead because he is more powerful than death (v 24).

- **How do people respond to Spirit-filled Christians?** • **v 12:** They are intrigued. They don't understand, but would like to.
  - **v 13:** They laugh at them.
  - **v 41:** They listen to what they say about Christ, and repent and are baptised (a public declaration of their new loyalty to Christ); they are forgiven and receive the Spirit ie: they become Christians.

7. APPLY: What are Jesus' followers on earth to do today? Take the message about him—who he is, what he's done and how people need to respond—to the "ends of the earth", wherever we are in that earth.

- **What are the key points of the witness statement we're to give about Jesus (v 22-24, 36, 38)?**
  - Who he is: a historical man, chosen by God as the Messiah, proved by miracles.
  - What he did: he died as part of God's plan, rejected by humanity. He rose again, triumphing over death.
  - How people need to respond: repent—turn back to God—and make a public declaration of loyalty to Jesus. This brings forgiveness and the gift of the Spirit.

- **How does Acts 1 v 8 encourage us to get on with doing this?** We have the Holy Spirit, God himself, working in us to enable us to do our part in this mission.

8. APPLY: How have you seen the three responses to the Christians in Acts 2 in your Christian life? Encourage people briefly to recount how they've: seen people be intrigued by how they live; been laughed at as a Christian; seen people listen to the gospel and turn to Jesus.

- **How does this encourage us to get on with living for and talking about Jesus?** Rejection and abuse aren't new! But alongside these, we see people being intrigued and asking questions, and even coming to faith. That was the experience of the first Christians, of giants such as Peter—we have the privilege of following in their footsteps. We don't need to worry if people laugh at and reject us, as long as we're living and speaking for Christ.

9. This is the first Christian church. What do we see here about what church is, and what church does?
- **v 42:** Church is a group of people who listen to the apostles' teaching (the New Testament, and the Old Testament on which they based their teaching about Jesus, just as Peter did in v 16-21).
- **v 42:** Church is about fellowship, a family.
- **v 42:** Church shares Communion and prays together.
- **v 43:** A church is full of awe at how God works (or, in our days, has worked) through the apostles he chose.
- **v 44-45:** Church members are united, and so we share everything we have, and are prepared to give up anything we have in order to support each other.
- **v 46:** Church is about meeting together publicly (as we do on Sundays), and regularly and privately (in homes—as we should throughout the week).

- **What is challenging about the word "devoted" in v 42?** This is the Spirit-inspired attitude Christians have to their church community. There is nothing half-hearted or moderate here. We are often tempted to hold back; to see church as something which gives, not something to which we give; to make church one of a number of equal priorities in life. The word "devoted" challenges these views.

10. What does verse 47 tell us about the way the Lord works through his people? Why is this exciting? Church is the way God works through his Spirit to save people. As a church praises God and serves one another, people see this, and God works to add them to his people. Why wouldn't being part of this be exciting?!

11. So far, we've seen God's Spirit-filled people witnessing about his Son in Jerusalem. Read these parts of Acts and trace the progress of the message about Jesus: You'll find each on the map on p 60.
- **8 v 1b-8:** Judea and Samaria
- **11 v 19-21:** Antioch, a major city
- **17 v 13-15, 32-34:** Thessalonica and Berea, large Greek towns (v 13); Athens, the Greek capital and centre of academia and philosophy in the ancient world
- **28 v 11-16, 30-31:** Rome, the capital of the greatest empire the world had seen, the centre of the known world.
- **How does Acts show God's people obeying his mission command from 1 v 8?** They take the gospel message from Jerusalem, from a handful of, and then a few thousand, believers, throughout the known world. **How does Acts show God's promise to Abram being fulfilled?** God had promised Abram (Gen 12 v 3) that the blessing of living as part of his people would come to "all peoples"; in Acts, we see this coming true, as people of many nations come to faith in Christ.

⊻
- **How does 8 v 1b-8 show God giving his people a surprising helping hand? What can we learn from this?** It's persecution that prompts Jesus' followers to move out from Jerusalem. God uses opposition to the gospel message to further the gospel message! Suffering as Christians isn't a sign things have gone wrong—in fact, God can use our suffering as we live for and speak about Jesus to further the mission he's given his people.

12. APPLY: What have we seen about the priorities Christians should have between Jesus' ascension and his return? (1) Being part of the way the news of Jesus reaches everywhere in the world. Mission is our priority. (2) Being devoted to fellow Christians. Church is our priority. **Note:** These priorities overlap, because part of the point of church is to tell people about the Lord; and as church members devote themselves to each other and their church, God will work to save outsiders who see how the church lives.

- **What can make it hard to have these priorities?** Many things! Our own hearts, which suggest there are other more important things to live for. Our lives, which are often busy with other things, so that church ends up being an optional extra. Those around us, who reject our message (and, sometimes, us) and laugh at our commitment to church. Even our churches themselves, where we can often frown on radical, sacrificial devotion, preferring to promote moderation and comfort. **How do Acts 1 and 2 help us and encourage us in our task?** We each have the Spirit's power, equipping us to do these things (1 v 8, 2 v 1-4); that Jesus will one day return (1 v 11); that as we speak of Jesus, though some mock, some will be saved (2 v 13, 41); that as we devote ourselves to our church, it will become the community of 2 v 42-46; that God uses devoted churches to save others (v 47). The group may want to focus on just a couple of these encouragements, or you can point them to particular verses to pick out the encouragements listed above.

SNAPSHOT

King Jesus is in heaven, with his Father. His people spread the gospel around the world.

EXPLORE MORE: Galatians 5 v 16-25
What fight is going on inside every Christian? One between "the flesh" or "the sinful nature" (how we naturally are, rebellious against God) and "the Spirit" (which lives in us because we have turned to God's Son as our King and Saviour).
What kind of things are examples of a lifestyle which is rebelling against King Jesus (v 19-21)? We naturally focus on the things in this list which we don't do, and

ignore or excuse the ones we do. Encourage your group to avoid doing this!
What does Jesus' Spirit work to replace those things with (v 22-24)? It's worth encouraging your group members to praise God for the fruits they can see growing in them, and pray for those they can't— perhaps choosing one in particular and thinking what this fruit would look like in their particular life.
How should Christ's followers try to live (v 16, 25)? By the Spirit, in step with the Spirit. The Spirit lives in us—but we need to strive, in fact to fight, to allow the Spirit to be our leader, rather than our sinful nature.
How do these verses challenge you? How do they encourage you? Let your group share one or the other, or both. One general encouragement and challenge is that the Christian life always involves an internal battle. If Christians feel they're in a constant conflict inside, and know they sometimes do the wrong thing, that's a sign that the Spirit is at work. A true Christian is battling hard—if we don't feel there's a conflict, then we're losing the battle.

9 Revelation 20 – 22
IN A PERFECT WORLD

BIG IDEA

Jesus' return will bring the perfect re-creation of this world, for him to live in with his people eternally—so keep going!

SUMMARY

We have reached the end of the Bible! This session focuses on the final 2 ½ chapters of Revelation, a vision given to Jesus' apostle, John, when he was a very old man in exile

on Patmos (today's Crete, 1 v 9). Much of Revelation is showing us the present age (between Jesus' ascension and return) from heaven's perspective. But the last few chapters focus on what will happen in the future, when Jesus returns.

The session focuses on seeing how what will happen when our Lord returns is the complete fulfilment of the whole of God's work, and promises, in history (see Q4+5).

In some ways, the Bible comes full circle—back to God living with his perfect people, who enjoy blessing under his perfect rule, in his flawless world. But, as Q7 helps us see, in many ways the eternal city of Revelation 21 – 22 is even better than the "very good" garden of Genesis 1 – 2. A helpful image is to think of the Scriptures coming full circle, but in the same way a spiral staircase does—in a way, back to the same place, but even higher.

The main "action point" of the whole book is to keep going in our faith, no matter how painful or difficult. With this promised life in this promised world to look forward to, guaranteed to us by our risen Lord and Saviour, we will be able to go through anything, and lose everything, in this life.

Note: It's worth pointing out to your group that Revelation is not the easiest book to understand down to the fine details, and that it is apocalyptic writing, so much of it is imagery. What we have to work hard at is seeing what realities the symbolism is picturing. For instance, hell is pictured as a "lake of fire" (20 v 14), outside God's new creation. We are not meant to ask whether it is literally a lake, and if so how it could be outside what God has made—we are simply supposed to see that hell is real, and awful.

This study does not deal with the whole of Revelation! And it does not deal with the details of exactly when Jesus will return, and whether his perfect world will come as he returns, some time after he returns, or is being formed before he returns. These questions of "millennialism" are ones Bible-believing Christians disagree over, and they are not the main concern either of Revelation or of this session!

OPTIONAL EXTRA

Draw sets of the eight "snapshots" we've covered so far. Split into pairs, with a set for each pair, and rearrange them in order, talking through what they symbolise as you go. Part of the idea of this Good Book Guide is that, in a few months' time, your group members can still remember the basic outline of the Bible story. Encourage them to try to memorise the snapshots, the titles of each session, and the promises made and kept (see Q10). If you do this activity at the end of this session, you can add the snapshot for this session too!

GUIDANCE TO QUESTIONS

1. For this world to become perfect, what would have to change? What would have to go? Allow people to give flippant answers—Mondays, or mobile phones, or soap operas! But other, more serious, answers may include: the human heart; death; war; pain and suffering; the devil; disappointment; unemployment; sin.

2. What is at the centre of this scene (20 v 11, 21 v 5)? A throne (white = pure) with someone seated on it who has power over creation and is making "everything new". On the throne is God: Father and Son.

3. What will God shut out of his world? Why is each of these "evictions" necessary if his world is to be made perfect?

- **20 v 14:** Death and Hades. Hades is Greek for "place of the dead". It's likely that John is underlining the point that there is no more death anymore—there is only existence in hell, or life with King Jesus.

- **20 v 12, 15; 21 v 8:** This is a little tricky—but basically, people. We will recognise ourselves in the "types" of people who face eviction from the world, and eternity in hell, in v 8—eg: all of us are idolators; almost all of us have been liars, too.

- **Look back to 20 v 10:** The devil, the beast and false prophet. This is Revelation-speak for all evil spiritual powers, including the most powerful, the devil.

- **21 v 4:** Tears, death, mourning, crying, pain—all signs that life isn't as it could be. One, death, is the end of life in this world.

4. Re-read 21 v 2-7. How is this future event the complete fulfilment of God's promises...

- **that creation will be "very good" (Genesis 1 v 31)?** The new heavens and the new earth are amazing, with nothing bad in them—"very good" is the minimum description required!

- **to Adam and Eve, of someone to crush the devil and conquer sin and death (Genesis 3 v 15)?** The devil, death and sin have all ended up in the lake of fire.

- **to Abraham, of a people in a land enjoying God's blessing (Genesis 12 v 1-3)?** This is the ultimate "place" where God blesses his people—drawn from all nations—as promised to Abram.

- **to David, of an everlasting, perfect ruler (2 Samuel 7)?** Jesus is seated on the throne at the centre of both judgment and renewal. In the new world he is the King, and recognised as the King, of everything.

- **to the prophets, of a wonderful future beyond judgment (eg: Amos 9 v 11-15)?** This is the place of peace, plenty and prosperity—unimaginable blessing—the prophets pictured for God's people after they had been judged. Of course, the ultimate, cosmic judgment on our sin was taken by Jesus, so that we would not have to suffer it eternally (see Session Six).

5. What does verse 15 suggest is the only way out of this eternal misery? By having our name in another book—in the "book of life". Only if our name is found there can we avoid hell.

- **Read 13 v 8; 21 v 27. This book belongs to "the Lamb who was slain"—Jesus. How is this the ultimate fulfilment of God's promise to Moses (see Session Four)?** Here is the Lamb whose people are rescued not from Egypt but from hell, whose people are taken not to the eastern Mediterranean seaboard but to a perfect world. The names of the people he died for are found in this "book"—and because their death has been taken by the Lamb, Jesus, they will not need to die eternally.

6. APPLY: ... How can we use Revelation 20 – 21 to encourage each other to keep going? Mainly by reminding each other, as well as ourselves, of what is coming in our future. Sometimes we need to have our horizons lifted from the busyness, or pain, or even success, of our daily lives here. We need to remember that what ultimately matters is reaching our home with Jesus.

- **Read 1 Thessalonians 4 v 13-18. What situation is Paul talking about here (v 13)?** A Christian believer dying.

- **Where does he point such grieving Christians (v 14-17)?** The day Jesus returns, those who died in the faith and the faithful who are alive are reunited, and we live for ever with him.

- **What does he command them, and us, to do (v 18)?** Tell each other these truths when we are grieving.

7. Compare this future eternal city to

God's original garden creation. How is it similar? How is it even better?

Garden	City
Gen 2 v 9: Tree of life	*Rev 22 v 1-2:* Tree of life (see Note below)
Gen 3 v 8a, 2 v 15-16: God is very present	*Rev 22 v 4a:* We will see God's face (wow!)
Gen 1 v 26-28: Made in God's image, to rule over his creation	*Rev 22 v 3b, 5b:* We will reign as God's servants
Gen 1 v 14-16: Sun created to give light	*Rev 22 v 5:* Light comes directly from God.

Note: In the garden, the tree of the knowledge of good and evil represented rule—so humans should not have eaten from it, because rule was reserved for the Creator God. But the man and woman chose to reject God's rule, taking the fruit themselves. In the city there will only be people who have definitively chosen to live under the rule of God and the Lamb—so this tree is replaced by his throne. He is the recognised, exalted Ruler. No one will choose to sin, because everyone there will have already, definitively, chosen to live under the loving rule of God's King.

• **How does this make you feel?** You may want to stop and pray at this point.

SNAPSHOT

Where it's all been heading: God's people in his perfect world, under his King's rule.

8. Read Revelation 1 v 12-19. This is the beginning of John's vision. How does it give us certainty that what he has written down is true? The vision is given to John by Jesus. And Jesus is all-powerful (don't get bogged down in the symbolism of v 12-16—the point is that Jesus is unimaginably majestic!). V 18 points us to the fact he "was dead, and … [is] alive for ever". The resurrection is where we can find certainty that this Jesus really does exist, and that this vision really is true and trustworthy. We find reassurance of this throughout Revelation (eg: 21 v 5; 22 v 6, 16, 20).

9. APPLY: What is one right response to knowing this is the future (22 v 20b)? "Amen"—this is true, I believe this, this will happen. "Come, Lord Jesus"—the greatest event of any Christian's life will be the day Jesus returns. **What difference will saying and meaning this make to life now?** This is what Christians are looking forward to and living for. It gives hope in difficult times, perspective in joy and mourning, motivation to share the gospel.

10. APPLY: Can you remember:
• **the title of each session (they're alphabetised!)?** See contents page.

• **the promises made in Sessions 1 – 6?** A very good world; a man to crush the devil; God's people from all nations living in his land, enjoying his blessing; deliverance from judgment through another taking that judgment; an everlasting King to lead us in obeying God; a wonderful future beyond our judgment (in Christ).

• **how Jesus is the way God keeps each promise in his first and second comings?** *He is the One* who began the re-creation when he came 2,000 years ago, and will finish it one day.

He is the One who crushed the devil on the cross by removing his claim on us as sinners, and will throw him into hell.
He is the One who makes us God's people, and who will bring us to God's ultimate perfect place of blessing.
He is the One who died in our place, taking God's judgment that we deserve.
He is the One who is the perfect Ruler, who leads his people in obeying God.
He is the One who, having taken our judgment, takes us to a place where we enjoy amazing blessings in this world.

EXPLORE MORE: 2 Peter 3 v 2-14
What will happen between Jesus' ascension and return (2 Peter 3 v 3-6)?
People will scoff at the idea he'll come back (v 3), saying nothing changes (v 4); they'll ignore the fact God has already judged the world once, in Noah's time (v 6, Gen 6 – 8).
How does Peter answer these "scoffers" (v 8, 10)? God's timing is not like our timing! What seems a long time to us does not to the Creator. The "day of the Lord" will come suddenly and without warning: so of course you can't predict it or see the world changing because it's on its way!
Why has the Lord not yet fulfilled his promise to return (v 9)? Because he is waiting for more and more people to repent and come under his rule, so that for them his return is good news, not terrifying.
What should the Lord Jesus Christ's followers do until he returns?
- **v 2:** Read and remember the Old Testament (prophets) and New Testament (apostles)—what you've been doing over these nine sessions!
- **v 11-13:** Live holy (distinctive, different and pure) and godly (like God) lives; look forward to and hope for God's return.
- **v 14:** Be "spotless" and "blameless" ie: living good lives and seeking to get rid of sinfulness; be at peace with God, in right relationship with him (through living under his rule and repenting when we don't).

You've had the Bible tour… now stop off and take your time!

OLD TESTAMENT
Genesis 1 – 4: In the beginning
7 studies. ISBN: 9781907377112

David: God's true king
6 studies. ISBN: 9781904889984

Ezekiel: The God of glory
6 studies. ISBN: 9781904889274

Jonah: The depths of grace
6 studies. ISBN: 9781907377433

NEW TESTAMENT
Mark 1 – 8: The coming King
10 studies. ISBN: 9781904889281

1 John: How to be sure
7 studies. ISBN: 9781904889953

Revelation 2 – 3: A message from Jesus to the church today
7 studies. ISBN: 9781905564682

Visit your local website to see the full Good Book Guide range, and to download samples
UK & Europe: www.thegoodbook.co.uk • North America: www.thegoodbook.com
Australia: www.thegoodbook.com.au • New Zealand: www.thegoodbook.co.nz

thegoodbook
COMPANY
Opening up the Bible

At The Good Book Company, we are dedicated to helping Christians and local churches grow. We believe that God's growth process always starts with hearing clearly what he has said to us through his timeless word—the Bible.

Ever since we opened our doors in 1991, we have been striving to produce resources that honour God in the way the Bible is used. We have grown to become an international provider of user-friendly resources to the Christian community, with believers of all backgrounds and denominations using our Bible studies, books, evangelistic resources, DVD-based courses and training events.

We want to equip ordinary Christians to live for Christ day by day, and churches to grow in their knowledge of God, their love for one another, and the effectiveness of their outreach.

Call us for a discussion of your needs or visit one of our local websites for more information on the resources and services we provide.

UK & Europe: www.thegoodbook.co.uk
North America: www.thegoodbook.com
Australia: www.thegoodbook.com.au
New Zealand: www.thegoodbook.co.nz

UK & Europe: 0333 123 0880
North America: 866 244 2165
Australia: (02) 6100 4211
New Zealand (+64) 3 343 1990

www.christianityexplored.org

Our partner site is a great place for those exploring the Christian faith, with a clear explanation of the good news, powerful testimonies and answers to difficult questions.

One life. What's it all about?